THE WH
GUIDE TO PENSIONS

ABOUT THE AUTHOR

Jonquil Lowe is a freelance financial journalist and former head of the Money Group at Consumers' Association. She is the author of several other books, including *The Which? Guide to Giving and Inheriting*.

THE WHICH?
GUIDE TO PENSIONS

JONQUIL LOWE

CONSUMERS' ASSOCIATION

Which? Books are commissioned and researched by
The Association for Consumer Research and published by
Consumers' Association, 2 Marylebone Road, London NW1 4DF

Distributed by The Penguin Group:
Penguin Books Ltd, 27 Wrights Lane, London W8 5TZ

First edition June 1993
Revised edition August 1994
Copyright © 1993 Consumers' Association Ltd

British Library Cataloguing in Publication Data
Lowe, Jonquil
"Which?" Guide to Pensions: Finding Your
Way Profitably Through the Pensions
Maze. – 2Rev.ed – ("Which?" Consumer Guides)
I. Title II. Series
331.25
ISBN 0 85202 521 1

Cover photographs by courtesy of ACE photo agency/Ross Vincent/
Christopher Fogg/Mauritius Bildagentur

Typeset by Litho Link Limited, Welshpool, Powys, Wales
Printed and bound by Firmin-Didot (France), Group Herissey,
N° d'impression: 27104

CONTENTS

INTRODUCTION

HAVING enough income for a comfortable retirement is a simple concept, but ensuring it in practice is not so easy. Pensions – whether provided by the state or direct from your own pocket – are expensive. And because you're dealing with what *might* happen in the future, there's no straightforward way of knowing whether your retirement savings are on target. Frequent changes to the rules and regulations concerning pensions and investments haven't helped: the whole subject is now so ridiculously complex that even the experts have trouble keeping track. You could be forgiven for turning your back on the whole complicated issue, but you simply cannot afford to do so.

State pensions alone are not enough to fund a reasonable standard of living. Perhaps you've contracted out of SERPS (the State Earnings Related Pension Scheme) and taken out a personal pension plan instead. But don't assume that will be sufficient either. Unless you make substantial additional savings through a personal plan or you belong to an employer's pension scheme, you are probably heading for an impoverished old age.

Choosing a pension, then, may be the most important piece of financial planning you'll ever undertake. But where do you start? How can you find out what money you'll eventually receive and what extra savings you might need to make now? Advice would be useful, but can you be sure that it will be expert, sound and impartial? *Which?* has consistently found problems with many financial advisers. And a review of client files for the Securities and Investments Board (SIB), in 1993, found that advice given to people who were transferring pension rights from an employer's scheme to a personal plan was '*suspect*' in nearly 60 per cent of cases and at least '*unsatisfactory*' in a further 22 per cent[1]. That's not to say that all these people have necessarily bought the wrong pension plan or lost money; until SIB has carried out further research, the number who have won't be known. But some estimates suggest that as many as 100,000 people may have lost out and will need to be compensated. More recently, a major insurance company has taken the drastic step of laying off all its pensions salespeople in order to retrain them after the industry regulator found shortcomings in the company's existing arrangements. None of this inspires confidence in the quality of advice you may get. Undoubtedly, there are sound advisers, but you need to be able to sort the wheat from the chaff. To do that, you'll have to develop a working knowledge of pensions, as well as knowing broadly what to expect from a good adviser.

The Which? Guide to Pensions will help. Chapter by chapter, with the aid of numerous examples, it:

- explains what you can expect to receive from the state and when
- tells you how contracting out is likely to affect your pension income and whether it's a good idea for you
- describes the pension and other benefits you can expect from an employer's scheme if you belong to one
- looks at the options open to you if you leave an employer's scheme before retirement
- details the way that personal pensions work and how you can use them
- helps you to ensure that your pension savings are safe.

However, at the end of the day, no book can tell you precisely what the right course of action is for you personally. If you decide that you need one-to-one advice, the book *can* tell you what your options are, how to find the type of adviser you need and how to tell if he or she is likely to be giving you the right advice.

[1] KPMG Peat Marwick survey for the Securities and Investments Board, 1993

When you reach retirement, you need to be sure of the nuts and bolts of tracing and claiming pensions due, perhaps, from several sources, so you'll find advice about that too. In short, this is a book for everyone who is concerned about their retirement income, whether they are just about to start saving, want to check up on their pensions to date or are on the brink of what should be a well-planned and enjoyable retirement.

The benefits and taxation details in this book are up-to-date as at March 1994 and take account of changes proposed in the November 1993 Budget. At the time of writing, the Budget proposals were still being debated by Parliament and could be altered before passing into law as the Finance Act 1994.

Note Addresses and telephone numbers for those organisations marked with an asterisk (*) can be found in the address section at the back of the book.

CHAPTER 1

YOUR RETIREMENT INCOME

Leisure at last

THANKS to advances in medicine, better diet and housing, and improved working conditions, you can expect to live to a ripe old age. Also, increased affluence means that many people can now choose when they want to retire rather than soldiering on until the state pension age. Retirement is no longer made up of a few twilight years but is a phase of life which can easily last two or even three decades, as you can see from Table 1.1 below.

Table 1.1: Average length of retirement

If you retire at age:	On average, you can expect this many years in retirement:	
	women	*men*
50	30	26
55	26	21
60	22	17
65	18	14
70	14	11
75	11	8
80	8	6
85	6	5

Source: *Government Actuary's Department*

Retirement is becoming a long and welcome period of life in which you have leisure to pursue hobbies, indulge your interests, return to studies or maybe even adopt a new career.

How much retirement income?

To make the most of retirement you need to have sufficient income. You're looking a long way ahead, so you can't be sure how much you'll need – you'll have to estimate how much income would be enough. Your estimate will be based on your likely *needs* in retirement and the type of lifestyle you *want*. Your income needs may be less in retirement than now if, say, you'll have paid off a mortgage, can save on travel to work, or will need one car in the family instead of two. On the other hand, needs could rise if, for example, you have to replace a car previously provided by your employer, or pay for meals that had been cheap, or free, at work.

No one likes to dwell on the gloomier side of life, but you must be realistic in your planning, so you should also consider needs which may arise later in retirement. Figures published by the government suggest that many people aged 75 or more are likely to have some special needs related to health:

Table 1.2: Coping with health problems in old age

| | People aged 75 and over | |
	Men	Women
Percentage of people admitted to hospital as in-patients in a twelve-month survey period	20	16
Percentage of people visiting the casualty or out-patient department of a hospital in a three-month survey period	22	20
Average number per person of visits to the doctor (NHS) in 1991	7	6
Average number per person of days when activity was restricted because of illness in 1991	54	58

Source: *General Household Survey 1991* London: HMSO, 1993

Therefore, you should plan on the basis that you may have to spend more on health care and, perhaps, cope with reduced mobility, which may require alterations and adaptations to your home, furniture, and so on. Eventually, you may prefer, or need, to give up your own house and move to a residential home, which, at 1994 prices, could cost at least £300 a week – although you might qualify for help from the state with these costs. You should consider now how you might meet such extra expense. You could set aside some savings specifically for use in later retirement. Alternatively, you might consider taking out various forms of insurance. For example, medical bills insurance can cover or pay towards private medical costs. Long-term care insurance is designed to pay out a regular sum if you require long-term care either at home or in a residential or nursing home or hospital. Ideally, you should make your plans for later retirement *now* and not on the eve of your retirement, when it may be too late to build up adequate savings and insurance may be too costly, or even impossible, to get.

As noted above, retirement planning is not just about needs. Wants are important too. You might want to spend more on your lifestyle once you retire: you might want to take up hobbies for which you didn't previously have time; you might want to travel more. If you travel a lot already, your spending might fall in retirement because you're likely to have the flexibility to travel at cheaper times.

You can fill in the expense calculator on pp.14 and 15 to give you a guide to your expected retirement spending. Write down your estimates in *today's* prices and values. The total gives you an idea – in today's money – of the after-tax retirement income that you'll require. In general, you'll need a lower *before-tax* income than now to finance your chosen lifestyle because older people qualify for higher tax-free allowances (see Chapter 18). But, if you decide to retire relatively early, this won't apply for the first few years.

Don't ignore inflation

It's not easy deciding how much you need to set aside for retirement. The problem is made more difficult because of the effect of inflation. Rising prices eat away at the buying power of your money. Even at the fairly low rates of inflation which Britain has experienced in recent years, prices will have risen alarmingly after a decade or two. And, if inflation returns to higher levels, the jump in prices will be even more devastating. Chart 1.1 below shows what inflation can do to the prices of everyday items:

Chart 1.1: Inflation in your shopping basket

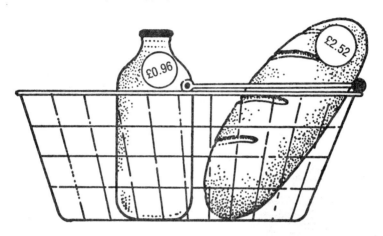

	milk (pint)		bread (large bloomer)	
	1994 price	27p	1994 price	71p
yearly inflation:	2%	5%	2%	5%
year				
2000	£0.30	£0.36	£0.80	£0.95
2010	£0.37	£0.59	£0.97	£1.55
2020	£0.45	£0.96	£1.19	£2.52

Inflation means that in future you'll need more £££ of income just to maintain the *same* standard of living as now. For example, even if today's low inflation rate of around 2 per cent a year continued, in 20 years' time you will need an income of nearly £15,000 to be able to buy the same amount that you can buy now with £10,000. Put another way, a yearly income of £10,000 today would then be worth only the same as £6,700 now, in terms of what it could buy 20 years ahead.

Expense calculator

Living at home

yearly total

Food shopping and household basics   £_____

Buying and repairing household equipment   £_____

Newpapers/magazines/books   £_____

TV licence/videos/music   £_____

Dog/cat/other pets   £_____

Clothes/shoes/cosmetics/hairdressing   £_____

Living it up

Sports and hobbies: materials/lessons/other   £_____

Dining out/theatre/cinema/concerts/exhibitions   £_____

Holidays/holiday home/second home   £_____

Other indulgences (e.g. smoking, drinking)   £_____

Transport

Owning a car: tax/insurance/servicing/repairs/
    breakdown insurance   £_____

Renting a car: rental charge/insurance   £_____

Running a car: petrol/oil/diesel   £_____

Train fares/bus fares/coach fares   £_____

Other travel costs   £_____

Home-related

Mortgage/rent   £_____

Repairs/service charge/decoration/furnishing   £_____

Building and contents insurance   £_____

Council tax/water rates   £_____

Gas/electricity/heating oil/solid fuel   £_____

Home help/window cleaner/other paid help   £_____

Gardening   £_____

Telephone   £_____

Health-related

Dentist   £_____

Optician   £_____

Hospital cash plan/private medical insurance   £_____

Long-term care insurance   £_____

Other health-related expenses   £_____

Caring for others

Spending on children/grandchildren   £_____

Financial help for elderly relatives   £_____

Christmas/birthday/other presents   £_____

Gifts to charity/church collections   £_____

Protection-type life insurance – see Chapter 9   £_____

Other caring expenses   £_____

Saving and borrowing

Saving to replace car, household equipment   £_____

Saving to finance home improvements   £_____

Saving to cover higher health spending later on   £_____

Other regular saving   £_____

Loan repayments (other than mortgage)   £_____

Other

Postage/stationery/other   £_____

TOTAL   £_____

Inflation affects both your savings for retirement and your income once you've retired. You need to invest your savings so that they'll stand a good chance of beating inflation, and you need to make sure that once your retirement income starts it will keep pace with inflation. But this isn't so easy because you don't know what the future rate of inflation will be. Table 1.3 below shows how different rates of inflation would affect the buying power of your money. For example, if inflation averaged two per cent a year for the next 35 years, the buying power of £1,000 would have been reduced to just £500. That seems bad enough, but if inflation averaged a higher rate of six per cent a year, your £1,000 would be worth just £130 in terms of what it could buy.

Table 1.3: How inflation could eat into your income
What £1,000 would be worth in future given different rates of inflation

| Years | Average yearly rate of inflation | | | | |
	2%	4%	6%	8%	10%
	£	£	£	£	£
1	980	962	943	926	909
2	961	925	890	857	826
3	942	889	840	794	751
4	924	855	792	735	683
5	905	822	747	681	621
10	820	676	558	463	386
15	743	555	417	315	239
20	673	456	312	215	149
25	610	375	233	146	92
30	552	308	174	99	57
35	500	253	130	68	36
40	453	208	97	46	22
45	410	171	73	31	14
50	372	141	54	21	9
60	305	95	30	10	3

Table 1.4 opposite looks at inflation from the other angle, and shows how many £££ you'll need in future to have the same buying power as £1,000 today, given different rates of inflation. You can use this table to convert the total in your expense calculator into the amount of £££, in terms of future price levels, that you expect to need when you retire – see the example which follows. As the expected pension from most schemes and plans is quoted in these terms, you can match up the answer you get with the pension you are forecast to receive at retirement.

Table 1.4: How many £££ you might need in the future
How much money you'd need in future, given different rates of inflation, for it to be worth the same as £1,000 today

Years	Average yearly rate of inflation				
	2%	4%	6%	8%	10%
	£	£	£	£	£
1	1,020	1,040	1,060	1,080	1,100
2	1,040	1,082	1,124	1,166	1,210
3	1,061	1,125	1,191	1,260	1,331
4	1,082	1,170	1,263	1,361	1,464
5	1,104	1,217	1,338	1,469	1,611
6	1,126	1,265	1,419	1,587	1,772
7	1,149	1,316	1,504	1,714	1,949
8	1,172	1,369	1,594	1,851	2,144
9	1,195	1,423	1,690	1,999	2,358
10	1,219	1,480	1,791	2,159	2,594
15	1,346	1,801	2,397	3,172	4,177
20	1,486	2,191	3,207	4,661	6,728
25	1,641	2,666	4,292	6,848	10,835
30	1,811	3,243	5,743	10,063	17,449
35	2,000	3,946	7,686	14,785	28,102
40	2,208	4,081	10,286	21,725	45,259
45	2,438	5,841	13,765	31,920	72,890
50	2,692	7,107	18,420	46,902	117,391
60	3,281	10,520	32,988	101,257	304,482

EXAMPLE 1.1

Jack, who's 35 now, would like to retire in the year 2024 at age 65 with an income equivalent to £15,000 a year in terms of today's (1994) money. If inflation averaged four per cent a year in the intervening 30 years, his income would need to be around £48,600 a year in terms of 2024 money. (If you use Table 1.4 above, find the figure in the 4% column and the 30-year row – i.e. £3,243. Multiplying this by 15 gives £48,645.) If inflation averaged 10 per cent a year, Jack's yearly income would need to start at £261,700 in 2024 money.

Sources of retirement income in the UK

There are four main sources of retirement income: pensions from the state, private pensions, income from investments and work you continue to do after retirement. Nearly half of all pensioners rely mainly on the state for their retirement income, and they make up many of the poorest pensioners. On their own, state pensions just don't provide enough to maintain a reasonable lifestyle – see Table 1.5. It's important to have other sources of retirement income too.

Table 1.5: Pensioners' incomes in 1992

Before-tax weekly income	Proportion of households receiving each level of income	
	All pensioner households	Pensioner households relying mainly on state pensions and other benefits
	%	%
Less than £60	10.7	24.0
£60 up to £79.99	16.2	34.0
£80 up to £99.99	11.3	13.9
£100 up to £129.99	12.9	17.1
£130 up to £159.99	10.6	6.8
£160 up to £199.99	9.7	2.4
£200 up to £239.99	6.4	1.2
£240 up to £279.99	5.6	0.5
£280 up to £319.99	4.5	0.1
£320 and over	12.1	0
TOTAL	100.0	100.0

Source: Derived from Family Expenditure Survey 1992 as reported in CSO *Family spending* London: HMSO, 1993

At present, the *average* pensioner household has an income of £175 a week. Nearly half of this comes from the state. An important way in which you can increase your expected retirement income is by building up your own retirement savings.

Chart 1.2: Where the money comes from

Each £1 of an average
pensioner's income is
made up of:

state pensions
and benefits   47p
private pensions   26p
investments   16p
work   10p
other   1p

Source: Family Expenditure Survey 1992 as reported in CSO *Family Spending* London:
HMSO, 1993

How the UK compares with the rest of Europe

In the UK, the state provides what might be described as a 'core
pension' – it aims only to provide a basic level of retirement
income, but most people would hope to supplement this with
income from other sources. Of the twelve countries which
make up the European Union (EU), there are five other
countries, besides the UK – Belgium, Denmark, Germany,
Ireland and the Netherlands – which take this 'core pension'
approach to the state scheme, although the generosity of the
state scheme varies. The private schemes in these countries
work in various ways but, basically, money paid in by
employers and employees is invested to provide enough to pay
out pensions to those employees when they eventually retire.

In Greece, Italy, Luxembourg and Portugal, private pension
schemes are rare. This was, until recently, the case in Spain too,
but private schemes are now becoming more widely used.

France operates an unusual scheme: the state scheme, which
provides a 'core pension', is supplemented by *compulsory*

industry-wide schemes to which employers and employees must contribute. Instead of the money paid into the compulsory schemes being saved up to pay future pensions, it is immediately paid out as pensions to people who are currently retired.

Table 1.6 shows roughly how much pension the state provides compared with pre-retirement earnings in each of the 12 member states and the extent to which private schemes are used. The figures apply only to 'eligible' earnings – commonly, earnings above a given level do not count for state pension purposes – and show the *maximum* which the state will replace. For example, you might think that UK state pensions don't seem too bad if they will replace half your earnings. But that is the *best* outcome – you may qualify for a lot less.

Table 1.6: Comparison of pensions in the EU countries

Country	State scheme replaces roughly this much of earnings	How widespread is the use of private pension schemes?
Belgium	Up to 60%	Extensive
Denmark	Up to 80%	Extensive
France	Up to 50%	Uncommon
Germany	Up to 50%	Extensive
Greece	Up to 100%	Uncommon
Ireland	Up to 65%	Extensive
Italy	Up to 80%	Uncommon
Luxembourg	Up to 70%	Uncommon
Netherlands	Up to 70%	Extensive
Portugal	Up to 80%	Uncommon
Spain	Up to 100%	Increasing
UK	Up to 50%	Extensive

Source: *Pensions in the European Community*, Clifford Chance, 1991

Building up your own pension

For most people in the UK, the best way of making their own savings for retirement is to use a specialised pension scheme or plan, since these benefit from several tax advantages:

- you get tax relief up to your highest rate of income tax on the amount you pay into a pension scheme or plan. For example,

if you're a basic rate taxpayer, paying £100 into a plan would cost you only £75, assuming a basic tax rate of 25 per cent
- your retirement savings build up free of any tax on income and capital gains
- when you eventually come to take your pension, it's taxable in the same way as your salary or wages have been, but you can usually take part of the proceeds of the scheme or plan as a tax-free lump-sum.

The snag with pension savings is that you can't draw them out before retirement, even in an emergency, though with many plans you can borrow on the strength of your retirement savings. In general, this means you need to be absolutely sure that money you set aside for retirement can be committed to long-term saving. On the other hand, you must be wary of putting off saving for retirement. Though other demands may seem more pressing, delaying, even for a few years, dramatically increases the amount of money you need to set aside. This is because the money you invest early has a long time to grow and makes a proportionately greater contribution towards your eventual pension than the money you invest later on. The example below shows how even a small delay can affect the amount you need to save.

EXAMPLE 1.2

Jack, who's 35 now, wants to retire at 65 on an income equivalent to £15,000 a year in today's money. If he had to provide all this himself, he'd need to build up a cash fund by retirement of around £214,000 in terms of today's money. This assumes that he could convert the cash fund into pension at the seven per cent rate, available at the time of writing, for an annuity guaranteed to increase by five per cent a year.

Assuming modest investment growth of one per cent a year more than the rate of inflation, Jack could build up that sum either by investing a lump sum of £159,000 now or £6,100, in today's money, each year from now until retirement. If he puts off saving for retirement, in five years' time he'd need to invest a lump sum of £167,000 or save £7,500 a year in today's money.

CHAPTER 2

YOUR PENSION CHOICES

HERE, we give a broad picture of the basic pension choices and guide you to the relevant chapters for details. Once you're familiar with the basics, you can go on to consider other aspects of your pension arrangements, such as what happens when you change jobs, what if you want to retire early, and so on. And pension schemes and plans usually provide benefits other than just a retirement pension for yourself – for example, life insurance and pensions for your widow or widower and children. These other aspects are covered in later chapters. In Chapter 19, we return to your main pension choices to summarise the factors you'll want to take into account in making your decisions.

Your most important sources of retirement income are likely to be a state pension and pensions that you build up privately. Nearly everyone who works builds up some **state basic pension**. If you're an employee, you can also build up **State Earnings Related Pension Scheme (SERPS) pension**, though you can opt out of this provided you have an alternative private pension arrangement, or be opted out of it if your employer runs a relevant private scheme. As long as you have earnings, you can build up your own pension, either through an **employer pension scheme** or **personal pension plan**. The particular choices that are open to you depend largely on whether you work for someone else or for yourself. Even if you're not currently working, there are steps you may be able to take to protect your pension position.

If you work for an employer

Your employer may run a pension scheme for which you're eligible. You can choose whether or not to join it and, if you already belong, you can leave if you like. Some employer schemes don't let you join if you're over a certain age, and some may put restrictions on you rejoining later on if you've chosen to leave – different schemes have different rules.

If you leave your employer scheme or you decide not to join it, or your employer doesn't run a scheme, you can – and, in most cases, should – make your own pension arrangements using a personal pension plan.

As an employee, you're covered by SERPS. If you join or already belong to an employer pension scheme, you may automatically be opted out of SERPS – in the jargon, you're **contracted out**. If this isn't the case, you can choose whether or not to contract out using a personal pension plan.

Chart 2.1 on pp.24 and 25 summarises your pension choices.

If you work for yourself

If you run your own business, you'll *have* to make your own private pension arrangements. If you're self-employed, you can do this using a personal pension plan. If your business is set up as a company, you have more choice: you could take out a personal pension plan but, instead, you could set up your own employer pension scheme. There are special **executive schemes** and **small self-administered schemes** which can be particularly useful for small companies.

If you're self-employed, you're not eligible for SERPS, so you can build up only a basic pension from the state – this means it's even more important that you consider making your own savings for retirement. If you're a director of your own company, you count as an employee, so you're covered by SERPS and you have the same choice about contracting out as any employee – see Chart 2.1.

Chart 2.2 on pp.26 and 27 summarises your pension choices.

Chart 2.1: Pension choices if you work for an employer

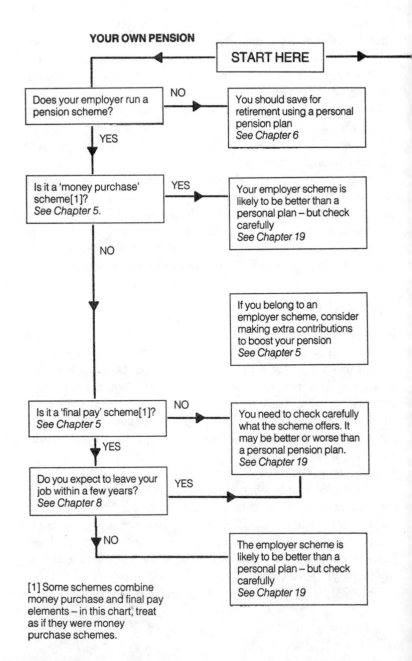

YOUR OWN PENSION

START HERE

Does your employer run a pension scheme? — **NO** → You should save for retirement using a personal pension plan
See Chapter 6

YES

Is it a 'money purchase' scheme[1]?
See Chapter 5. — **YES** → Your employer scheme is likely to be better than a personal plan – but check carefully
See Chapter 19

NO

If you belong to an employer scheme, consider making extra contributions to boost your pension
See Chapter 5

Is it a 'final pay' scheme[1]?
See Chapter 5 — **NO** → You need to check carefully what the scheme offers. It may be better or worse than a personal pension plan.
See Chapter 19

YES

Do you expect to leave your job within a few years?
See Chapter 8 — **YES** →

NO

The employer scheme is likely to be better than a personal plan – but check carefully
See Chapter 19

[1] Some schemes combine money purchase and final pay elements – in this chart, treat as if they were money purchase schemes.

YOUR STATE PENSION

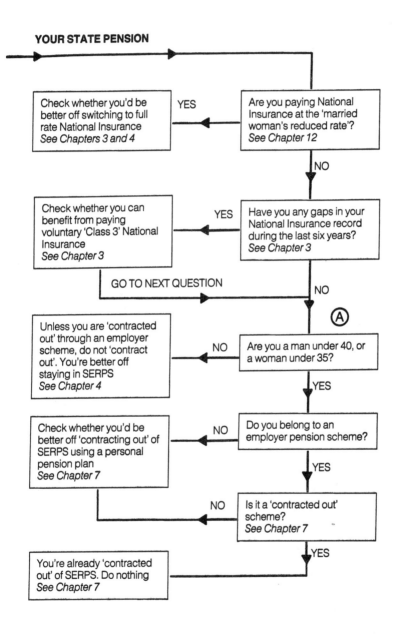

Check whether you'd be better off switching to full rate National Insurance
See Chapters 3 and 4

YES

Are you paying National Insurance at the 'married woman's reduced rate'?
See Chapter 12

NO

Check whether you can benefit from paying voluntary 'Class 3' National Insurance
See Chapter 3

YES

Have you any gaps in your National Insurance record during the last six years?
See Chapter 3

GO TO NEXT QUESTION

NO

Ⓐ

Unless you are 'contracted out' through an employer scheme, do not 'contract out'. You're better off staying in SERPS
See Chapter 4

NO

Are you a man under 40, or a woman under 35?

YES

Check whether you'd be better off 'contracting out' of SERPS using a personal pension plan
See Chapter 7

NO

Do you belong to an employer pension scheme?

YES

Is it a 'contracted out' scheme?
See Chapter 7

NO

YES

You're already 'contracted out' of SERPS. Do nothing
See Chapter 7

Chart 2.2: Your pension choices if you work for yourself

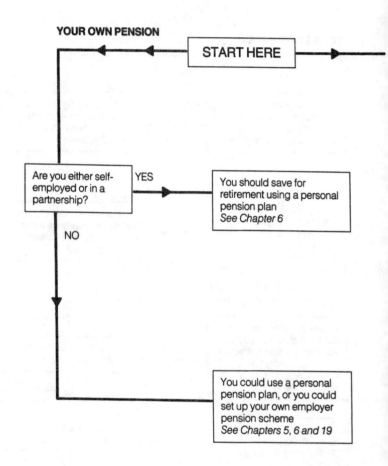

YOUR STATE PENSION

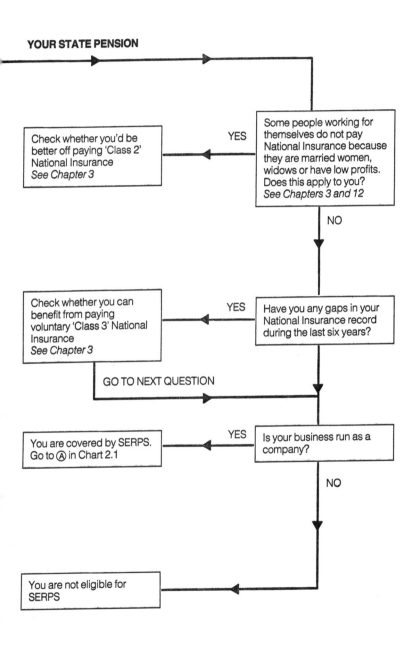

Some people working for themselves do not pay National Insurance because they are married women, widows or have low profits. Does this apply to you?
See Chapters 3 and 12

YES → Check whether you'd be better off paying 'Class 2' National Insurance
See Chapter 3

NO ↓

Have you any gaps in your National Insurance record during the last six years?

YES → Check whether you can benefit from paying voluntary 'Class 3' National Insurance
See Chapter 3

GO TO NEXT QUESTION

Is your business run as a company?

YES → You are covered by SERPS. Go to Ⓐ in Chart 2.1

NO ↓

You are not eligible for SERPS

Chart 2.3: Your pension choices if you're not working

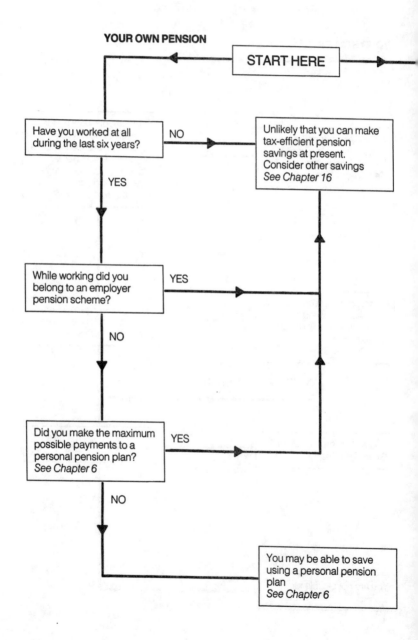

YOUR OWN PENSION

START HERE

Have you worked at all during the last six years? — NO → Unlikely that you can make tax-efficient pension savings at present. Consider other savings *See Chapter 16*

YES

While working did you belong to an employer pension scheme? — YES →

NO

Did you make the maximum possible payments to a personal pension plan? *See Chapter 6* — YES →

NO

You may be able to save using a personal pension plan *See Chapter 6*

YOUR STATE PENSION

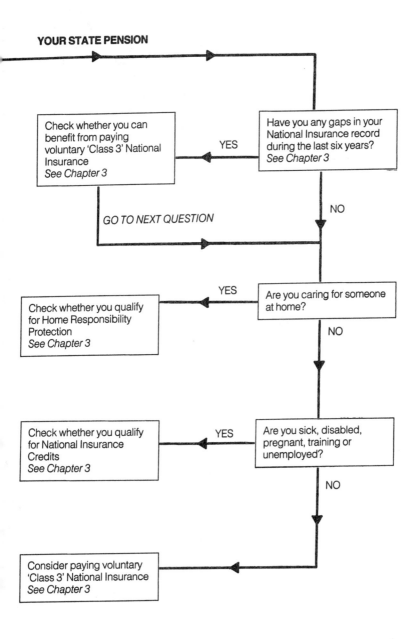

Check whether you can benefit from paying voluntary 'Class 3' National Insurance
See Chapter 3

YES

Have you any gaps in your National Insurance record during the last six years?
See Chapter 3

NO

GO TO NEXT QUESTION

Check whether you qualify for Home Responsibility Protection
See Chapter 3

YES

Are you caring for someone at home?

NO

Check whether you qualify for National Insurance Credits
See Chapter 3

YES

Are you sick, disabled, pregnant, training or unemployed?

NO

Consider paying voluntary 'Class 3' National Insurance
See Chapter 3

If you're not working

If you're not currently employed, your pension choices are limited. However, you should check your position with regard to the state pension – you may still be building up basic pension and, if not, you may be able to make sure that you do. You may also have scope to build up your own personal pension, if you've been earning during the last six years.

Chart 2.3 on pp.28 and 29 indicates the action you should take to check your position and summarises the pension choices that may be open to you – at least in theory. However, if money is tight you might find it hard, or even impossible, to put theory into practice.

CHAPTER 3

THE STATE BASIC PENSION

OVER ten million pensioners receive a flat-rate basic pension from the state. For half of them, this, together with other social security benefits, is their only income; for many others, the basic pension provides the backbone of their retirement finances.

How much pension?

Basic pension is paid at a full rate of £57.60 a week for a single person in the 1994–95 **tax year** (a tax year runs from 6 April to the following 5 April). A married couple can qualify for a higher pension of £92.10 a week, which is based on the husband's pension entitlement. If both partners qualify for a full basic pension in their own right, they can each receive the single rate, giving them 2 × £57.60 = £115.20 a week in total. The equivalent yearly amounts are shown in Table 3.1 over, together with the amounts for the previous seven years. You can see that the pension has increased each year. At present, basic pensions are increased each April at least in line with price inflation (measured by the yearly change in the Retail Prices Index up to the previous September). State retirement pensioners also qualify for a £10 bonus each Christmas.

Who qualifies?

You qualify for state basic pension by building up a sufficient record of **National Insurance**. National Insurance is a tax paid

Table 3.1: Yearly rates of state basic pension[1]

year	Single person £	Married couple £	Couple both with single pension £
1994–95	2,995.20	4,789.20	5,990.40
1993–94	2,917.20	4,669.60	5,834.40
1992–93	2,815.80	4,508.40	5,631.60
1991–92	2,704.00	4,329.00	5,408.00
1990–91	2,438.80	3,905.20	4,877.60
1989–90	2,267.20	3,629.60	4,534.40
1988–89	2,139.80	3,426.80	4,279.60
1987–88	2,054.00	3,289.00	4,108.00

[1] Excluding the Christmas bonus

by nearly everyone who works. If you don't work, you may be given National Insurance credits, or have your record protected in another way.

If you work for an employer

You pay **Class 1 National Insurance** provided your earnings are equal to, or more than, a **lower earnings limit**. The lower earnings limit is set by the government each year and is £57 a week, or its equivalent (for example, £247 a month or £2,964 a year) for the 1994–95 tax year. National Insurance on earnings up to the lower limit is charged at a rate of two per cent of those earnings, and counts towards the state basic pension. On earnings above the lower earnings limit, you pay National Insurance at a rate of 10 per cent from 1994–95, but only on earnings up to an upper earnings limit (see p.52). Your employer pays National Insurance in respect of *all* your earnings at one of several rates, the highest being 10.2 per cent.

If you earn less than the lower earning limit you don't pay National Insurance and you're not building up state basic pension. Married women who have opted to pay a special low rate of National Insurance are not building up a basic pension either – see Chapter 12.

If you work for yourself

If you're self-employed, you build up basic pension by paying **Class 2 National Insurance** at a flat rate – £5.65 a week in the 1994–95 tax year – and may also pay **Class 4 National Insurance**, but this doesn't count towards any state pensions or benefits.

If your profits are lower than a given limit – £3,200 for the 1994–95 tax year – you can choose not to pay Class 2 National Insurance. And, in the past, married women could choose not to make Class 2 payments, whatever their profits. This latter option was withdrawn from 6 April 1977, but if you'd already made this choice you can continue not to pay – see Chapter 12. In both these cases, you're not building up state retirement pension so you might be better off paying Class 2 National Insurance after all.

Since 6 April 1975, if you're a director of your own company, you count as an employee and you build up basic pension by paying Class 1 National Insurance as described on p.32.

If you're not working

In some situations, you may be credited with National Insurance, even though you haven't paid it. This happens:

- if you're claiming certain state benefits, such as unemployment, maternity or sickness benefit
- if you're a man within five years of state pension age (see p.35) and unemployed – you get the credits without having to 'sign on'
- for the years in which you have (or had) your sixteenth, seventeenth and eighteenth birthdays, if you were still at school and were born after 5 April 1957
- for the years in which you take part in an approved training course (but this doesn't include going to university), if you were born after 5 April 1957.

If you stay at home to care for your children, or a sick or elderly relative, you may qualify for **Home Responsibilities Protection** (HRP). Instead of getting credits, this protection reduces the length of National Insurance record that you need in order to qualify for a given level of basic pension. Under current rules, HRP can cover up to 19 years if you're a woman and up to 24 years if you're a man. You can get HRP automatically if you're receiving child benefit. In other cases, you'll usually need to claim it (see p.42).

If you don't qualify for credits or Home Responsibilities Protection, you may be able to pay voluntary **Class 3 National Insurance** in order to prevent there being a gap in your record. You can also use Class 3 payments to fill in earlier gaps in your record during the last six years. But you can't pay Class 3 National Insurance for any period when you had taken up the married women's option to pay National Insurance at the reduced rate or not at all.

Class 3 National Insurance is paid at a flat rate – £.5.55 each week in the 1994–95 tax year.

EXAMPLE 3.1

Megan left school aged 18 and went to university for three years. She is now 25 and earning a good salary working for a firm of stockbrokers in London. She has National Insurance credits for the tax years in which she reached ages 16, 17 and 18, and she now makes Class 1 payments. But there is a gap in Megan's record for the three years she was at college. She could fill this by paying voluntary Class 3 National Insurance, but she shouldn't delay doing this much longer: after this year, she won't be able to pay contributions for the year in which she was 19 because it will be more than six years ago. Megan can still make good the contributions for the years in which she reached ages 20 and 21.

Paid too little National Insurance?

Whether or not you qualify for the full rate of basic pension depends on your record of National Insurance. If you have too few contributions, you may qualify for a reduced-rate pension. If you've paid National Insurance for only a handful of years, you might not get any basic pension at all.

Table 3.2: Do your contributions count towards basic pension?

Type of contribution	Description	Do they count?
Class 1 – full rate	paid by employees (and their employers), including company directors [1], but not people earning less than the lower earnings limit	YES
Class 1 – reduced rate	paid by some married women and widows. (They can choose to switch to full rate – see Chapter 12)	NO
Class 2	paid by self-employed. Optional for people with profits below a given limit, and for some married women and widows	YES
Class 3	voluntary	YES
Class 4	paid by self-employed with profits above a given amount	NO

[1] Before 6 April 1975, company directors counted as self-employed

The appendix at the end of this chapter explains in detail how you qualify for the full-rate pension, and how a reduced-rate pension is calculated. You don't need to work this out for yourself, you can ask the DSS – see p.42.

When is basic pension paid?

State retirement pensions are payable from the **state pension age**, which is currently 60 for women and 65 for men. Where a wife's pension is based on her husband's National Insurance record, it can't be paid before the husband reaches age 65. If the wife is then under age 60, the husband will receive the extra pension in respect of her, provided she does not earn more than a given unit – £45.45 a week in 1994–95. Any employer's pension she receives counts as earnings for this purpose. If your wife is aged 60 or over, the extra pension will be paid directly to her and won't be affected by any earnings or other pension she gets. You can, of course, retire before you reach state pension age, but you'll have to make do without the state pension until you reach 60 or 65, as applicable.

You can put off starting to receive state pension for up to five years at present. Your eventual pension will be increased during that time by 7.5 per cent for each year you put it off. You can't defer taking state pension for longer than five years, as it becomes automatically payable at age 65 for women and age 70 for men. If you're under that age but you've already started to receive your pension, you can stop taking the pension and, thus, qualify for the increase until you reach 65 or 70, as applicable.

Suppose you decide to put off taking your pension for five years – will it be a good deal? If you gave up a full basic pension for the 1994–95 tax year, you'd lose £57.60 a week or £3,005.20 (including the Christmas bonus) for the year. Next year, you'd give up a bit more because the pension is increased each year to keep pace with inflation. But, if we look at the *buying power* of the pension you'd give up (and ignore extra increases to compensate for VAT on fuel bills), next year you'd also lose £3,005.20 in terms of 1994–95 money. If you gave up the pension for five years, you'd lose 5 × £3,005.20 = £15,026 in terms of 1994–95 money. At the end of five years, you'd start to receive your pension, but at an increased rate. The increase would be 7.5 per cent for each of the five years, which comes to 37.5 per cent (the yearly increase is not **compounded**, meaning that the increase earned for one year is not itself increased in the following years). Still working in terms of 1994–95 money, the increase in your basic pension would be 37.5% × £57.60 = £21.60 a week, or £1,123.20 a year. Dividing the £15,026 that you gave up by the £1,123.20 which you gain each year tells you how many years it will take until you've received as much pension as you gave up. The answer is 13⅓ years. A single man who starts to receive his deferred pension at age 70 would have to survive until age 83 to break even, but the life expectancy of the average 70-year-old man is only 11 years (see p.10). A woman starting to receive her deferred pension at age 65 would have to survive until age 78 to break even. She's likely to do this, because the life expectancy of the average 65-year-old woman is

18 years (see p.10). Other things being equal, deferring your pension for five years will generally appear worthwhile for a woman, but not for a single man.

The position for a married man is not clear-cut because, even after his death, his wife (assuming she outlives him) would continue to benefit from the increased amount of pension (see Chapter 9). How long the widow might, on average, be expected to benefit would depend on her age at the time of her husband's death.

Whether or not deferring your pension will be worthwhile will also depend on your relative tax rates both at the time you would give up the pension and at the time you would start to receive it again. If you expect your tax rate to fall in future, then deferring pension now to earn a higher rate later on is likely to be a good idea.

Finally, bear in mind that the discussion above has considered the position of an *average* man or woman, If your health is poor, you are less likely to benefit from deferring your pension.

Government figures show that, in practice, fewer than two per cent of pensioners do choose to defer their state pension.

EXAMPLE 3.2

Iain, a confirmed bachelor, will be 65 in three months' time. He runs his own business and doesn't intend to stop working yet, so he's thinking that he might put off taking his state pension for a while. He'd be giving up £3,005 a year, in terms of today's money. In return, once his pension started to be paid, it would be well over a third higher than the normal rate of pension – just over £79 a week instead of £57.60, in today's money. But that's not as tempting as it might seem: he'd need to be aged 83 before he'd received more pension than he gave up. Iain would need to live significantly longer than is average for a man of his age in order to profit from deferring his pension. He decides not to defer his pension. Instead, he starts to receive it at age 65, and uses it to bring forward spending on maintaining and improving his house.

EXAMPLE 3.3

Anne will be 60 in two months' time but will be able to carry on with her job for up to five more years. As she won't have to rely on her state pension immediately, she had been planning to invest it – for example, in unit trusts – to build up a capital sum to provide her with extra income later on when she finally stops work. But she would probably do better to tell the DSS not to pay her pension yet. To match the extra pension that deferment is guaranteed to give her, the unit trusts would need to grow by about 6.5 per cent a year (compounded) *on top of inflation*, given the current level of annuity rates – not impossible, but there is a fairly high risk that the return would fall short of this.

You don't have to retire in order to qualify for state pension. Basic pension used to be reduced if it was paid to you but you earned above a certain amount during the first five years after reaching state pension age. Since 1 October 1989, this has no longer been the case: the amount of your state pension is now unaffected by any earnings you have after reaching pension age.

Changes on the way

If you are a woman who was born after 5 April 1950, there are changes due to be made to the state pension system which will affect you. The government also plans some related changes which will affect everyone.

The background to change

The state pension age for women has been five years lower than the age for men since 1940. At that time, the lower age for women reflected the fact that wives tended to be younger than their husbands and that, being less likely themselves to work, they were usually reliant on their husbands for their retirement income.

As social conditions have changed – in particular, as more women have taken up careers – there has been much debate about whether it is fair for women to continue getting their pension from an earlier age than men, especially when women can expect to live a good deal longer anyway (see p.10). These two factors both make providing a pension for a woman more expensive than providing the same pension for a man, yet men and women pay the same rates of National Insurance.

This debate has been timely from the government's point of view. Looking ahead to the next century, the cost of state pensions looks set to double in real terms, largely due to an increasing number of pensioners. At the same time, the number of people of working age is set to fall. The government argues that, if nothing is done, taxes paid by working people to provide state pensions for those who have retired will need to increase sharply next century. Raising women's pension ages is one way of easing the problem.

The issue was brought to a crisis in 1990, when the European court ruled in a case called *Barber v Guardian Royal Exchange* (the 'Barber case') that employer pension schemes must offer equal pension terms and benefits for men and women. At the time, it was not precisely clear what the court meant by 'equal' but the writing was on the wall: some time soon it would be illegal for employer schemes to set separate pension ages for men and women. (See Chapter 12 for more about the Barber case and subsequent developments.)

The majority of employer schemes have, since the judgment, equalised their pension ages for men and women, if they did not already do this, and the most popular age chosen has been 65. But many employer schemes – particularly the larger ones – are designed to work in combination with the state pension scheme through the system of 'contracting out' (see Chapter 7). It quickly became clear that this could not continue unless either:

- the link between employer and state schemes was altered; or
- the state pension ages for men and women were also equalised.

In fact, it looks as if the government will act on both these fronts. It has already announced its plans to raise women's state pension age to 65 to match the current men's age (see over). However, these plans won't start to come into effect until 2010, so the government is also exploring ways of changing the link between the state and employers' schemes.

Changes affecting women born after 5 April 1950

If you are a woman who was born on or before 5 April 1950, you will still reach state pension age at age 60. If you were born after 5 March 1955, your state pension age is to be raised by five years to 65 – the same as the age for men. For women born between these dates, the pension age will be increased progressively until it reaches 65.

If you are caught in the transition period affecting women born between April 1950 and March 1955, you can calculate your state pension age according to this formula: 60 plus one month for each month (or part month) that your birth date falls after 5 April 1950. For this purpose, a month runs from the sixth day of one month to the fifth day of the next. Table 3.3 gives some examples.

Like men under the current rules (see p.33), once pension ages are equalised, women will automatically be credited with

Table 3.3: Pension age for women born between April 1950 and March 1955

Date of birth	Your state pension age	Date from which you'll get state pension
6 April 1950	60 years 1 month	6 May 2010
5 May 1950	60 years 1 month	6 May 2010
6 May 1950	60 years 2 months	6 July 2010
6 October 1950	60 years 7 months	6 May 2011
31 March 1951	61 years	6 March 2012
10 December 1951	61 years 9 months	6 September 2013
15 June 1952	62 years 3 months	6 September 2014
30 November 1952	62 years 8 months	6 July 2015
22 February 1953	62 years 11 months	6 January 2016
1 August 1953	63 years 4 months	6 November 2016
8 January 1954	63 years 10 months	6 November 2017
19 July 1954	64 years 4 months	6 November 2018
25 September 1954	64 years 6 months	6 March 2019
5 March 1955	64 years 11 months	6 January 2020
5 March 1955	65 years	6 March 2020

Source: Department of Social Security *Equality in State Pension Age* December 1993

National Insurance from age 60 to 65 if they are not working. So, for example, if a woman chooses to retire at the old pension age of 60, she will still be building up entitlement to the basic pension which will start to be paid once she reaches 65.

Changes affecting everyone
There are a number of other changes which are to be made at the same time as equalising the state pension ages for men and women. Most important of these are:

- at present, a husband can claim extra pension for a dependent wife but not vice versa (see p.35). When pension ages are the same, the extra pension for a dependant will be claimable by either the husband or the wife, depending on who reaches age 65 first. As now (see p.35), the amount of extra pension will be affected by any earnings or pension which the dependent spouse receives
- it will still be possible to earn extra pension by deferring your state pension (see p.36), but the terms will be different – you will be able to earn an extra 10 per cent pension for each year you put off receiving it and you will be able to defer for as many years as you like (rather than just five as at present)
- Home Responsibilities Protection (see p.33), which reduces the length of National Insurance contribution record you need for any given level of basic pension, will cover a maximum of 22 years for both men and women.

More information

Your main source of information about state pensions is the **Department of Social Security (DSS)**. You can find out where your nearest DSS office – also known as a **Benefits Agency** – is by looking in the telephone book under 'Social Security, Department of' or 'Benefits Agency'.

Benefits Agencies can either answer your questions or pass on your queries to the relevant section. If you have a general query, rather than one specific to your particular case, you can get information by telephoning DSS Freeline Social Security*. (The Freeline service is also available in some languages other than English – see p.242 for the relevant telephone numbers.)

Table 3.4: State basic pension: useful DSS leaflets

Leaflet number	Leaflet name
NP18	Class 2 and Class 4 NI contributions
NP28	National Insurance for employees
NP46	A guide to state retirement pensions
SA29	Your social security and pension rights in the European Community
NI1	National Insurance for married women
NI27A	National Insurance for people with small earnings from self-employment
NI35	National Insurance for company directors
NI42	National Insurance: voluntary contributions
NI48	National Insurance: late and unpaid contributions
NI51	National Insurance for widows
NI95	National Insurance for divorced women
NI125	Training for further employment and your National Insurance record
NI196	Social Security benefit rates and NI contribution rates
FB6	Retiring?
FB30	Self-employed?
FB31	Caring for someone?
CF411	Home Responsibilities Protection

Your local Benefits Agency will handle any claims that you make, supply forms that you need, and is a source of information leaflets. You can also order DSS leaflets from the DSS Leaflets Unit*. Table 3.4 above lists DSS leaflets that you may find particularly useful when you're considering your state basic pension entitlement.

The DSS runs a **Retirement Pensions Forecast and Advice (RPFA)** service which will provide you with details of the state pension you've built up so far, and your expected pension at retirement if your circumstances continue unchanged. The service will also indicate any steps that you could take to increase your entitlement – for example, paying Class 3

National Insurance to fill in gaps, or switching from the married women's reduced rate to full rate Class 1 payments. It gives you details and forecasts of your basic pension and also any state earnings related and graduated pensions (see Chapter 4) for which you qualify. You're allowed to have up to one forecast a year. To use the service, get Form BR19 from any DSS office, complete it and send it to the address given on the form. Expect to wait several weeks for a reply.

APPENDIX TO CHAPTER 3

How you qualify for basic pension

Do you have enough National Insurance each year?

How much pension you get depends on how many **qualifying years** of National Insurance you have. A 'qualifying year' is generally a tax year in which you've paid the required National Insurance. It's possible to pay some National Insurance during a year but not enough for that year to count towards your pension. Table 3.5 below shows how many contributions you need for a year to count towards your basic pension. A qualifying year doesn't have to be made up of payments all of the same type; you could, for example, have a mixture of Class 1 and Class 3 National Insurance, or Class 2 and Class 1. A Class

Table 3.5: How much National Insurance makes a qualifying year[1]

Type of payment	How many payments are needed for a tax year to count towards basic pension
Class 1	payments on earnings equal to, or more than, 52 times the weekly lower earnings limit
Class 2	52 payments
Class 3	52 payments

[1] The information in this table applies from 6 April 1975, except for Class 1 National Insurance where it applies from 6 April 1978. Up to 5 April 1975, both employees (except those on low earnings) and the self-employed paid National Insurance at a single rate. All these payments are added together and divided into 'lots' of 50. Each 'lot' counts as a year's worth of National Insurance, as does any remaining part-'lot'. From 6 April 1975 to April 1978, Class 1 payments on earnings of at least 50 (not 52) times the lower earnings limit were enough for the year to count towards the basic pension

1 payment on earnings equal to the weekly lower earnings limit is equivalent to one Class 2 or Class 3 payment.

Do you have enough qualifying years in your working life?

If at least 90 per cent of the years in your **working life** are qualifying years, you should get the full basic pension. If you have fewer qualifying years, you'll normally get a reduced rate of pension. But, if fewer than a quarter of the years in your working life are qualifying ones, you might not be entitled to any basic pension at all.

Table 3.6: How much state basic pension you'll get[1]

Number of years which are qualifying and count towards your state basic pension	Percentage of the full basic pension for which you qualify	
	women born before 6 April 1950	all men and those women born after 5 March 1955
9 or less	0	0
10	26	0
11	29	25
12	31	28
13	34	30
14	36	32
15	39	35
16	42	37
17	44	39
18	47	41
19	49	44
20	52	46
21	54	48
22	57	50
23	59	53
24	62	55
25	65	57
26	67	60

[1] If your working life is shorter than 44 years (women born before 6 April 1950) or 49 years (men and those women born after 5 March 1955), this table does not apply. See instead pp.46–50

Table 3.6 (contd)

Number of years which are qualifying and count towards your state basic pension	Percentage of the full basic pension for which you qualify	
	women born before 6 April 1950	all men and those women born after 5 March 1955
27	70	62
28	72	64
29	75	66
30	77	69
31	80	71
32	83	73
33	85	75
34	88	78
35	90	80
36	93	82
37	95	85
38	98	87
39	100	89
40	100	91
41	100	94
42	100	96
43	100	98
44 or more	100	100

'Working life' is an official definition. For most people, it means the tax years from the one in which you reach age 16 up to the last complete tax year before you reach pension age. Most men have a working life of 49 years and most women born before 6 April 1950 have a working life of 44 years. Your working life may be shorter than this if you were born before 5 July 1932. In this case, you should read the section *If you are older* on p.50. If you are a woman born after 5 March 1955, your working life will be 49 years – the same as for men.

Table 3.6 on p.45 and above shows what percentage of the full basic pension you'll get, depending on the number of qualifying years you've built up and assuming that your working life is 44 years if you're a woman, or 49 years if you're a man.

Chart 3.1: How long is your working life?

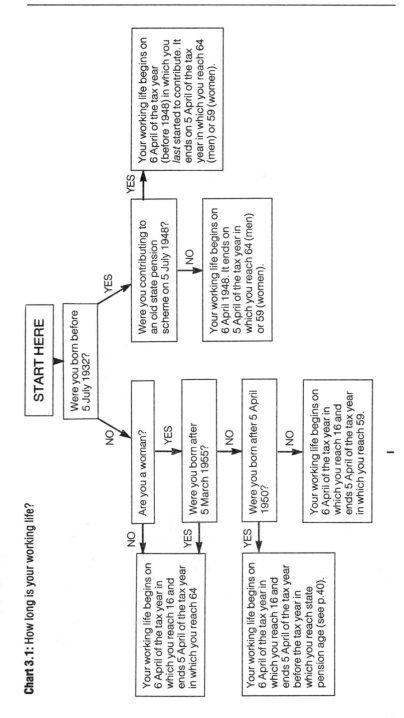

START HERE

Were you born before 5 July 1932?

YES → Were you contributing to an old state pension scheme on 5 July 1948?

YES → Your working life begins on 6 April of the tax year (before 1948) in which you *last* started to contribute. It ends on 5 April of the tax year in which you reach 64 (men) or 59 (women).

NO → Your working life begins on 6 April 1948. It ends on 5 April of the tax year in which you reach 64 (men) or 59 (women).

NO → Are you a woman?

YES → Were you born after 5 March 1955?

YES → Your working life begins on 6 April of the tax year in which you reach 16 and ends 5 April of the tax year before the tax year in which you reach state pension age (see p.40).

NO → Were you born after 5 April 1950?

YES → Your working life begins on 6 April of the tax year in which you reach 16 and ends 5 April of the tax year in which you reach 59.

NO (Are you a woman?) → Your working life begins on 6 April of the tax year in which you reach 16 and ends 5 April of the tax year in which you reach 64.

47

Chart 3.2: How much basic pension you're entitled to as a percentage of the full rate

Number of years in working life

	27	28	29	30	31	32	33	34	35	36	37	38	39	40	41	42	43	44	45	46	47	48	49
1																							
2																							
3																							
4	25	25																					
5	29	28	27	26	25	25																	
6	33	32	31	30	29	28	27	26	25	25													
7	37	35	34	33	32	31	30	29	28	27	27	26	25	25									
8	40	39	37	36	35	34	33	32	31	30	29	28	28	27	26	26	25	25					
9	44	42	41	40	38	37	36	35	34	33	32	31	30	30	29	28	27	27	26	26	25	25	
10	48	46	44	43	41	40	39	38	37	36	35	34	33	32	31	30	30	29	28	28	27	27	26
11	51	50	48	46	45	43	42	41	40	38	37	36	35	35	34	33	32	31	31	30	29	29	28
12	55	53	51	50	48	46	45	44	42	41	40	39	38	37	36	35	34	34	33	32	31	31	30
13	59	57	55	53	51	50	48	47	45	44	43	42	41	40	39	38	37	36	35	34	34	33	32
14	62	60	58	56	54	53	51	50	48	47	45	44	43	42	41	40	39	38	37	36	36	35	34
15	66	64	62	60	58	56	54	52	51	50	48	47	46	45	43	42	41	40	40	39	38	37	36
16	70	67	65	63	61	59	57	55	54	52	51	50	48	47	46	45	44	43	42	41	40	39	38
17	74	71	68	66	64	62	60	58	57	55	54	52	51	50	48	47	46	45	44	43	42	41	40
18	77	75	72	70	67	65	63	61	60	58	56	55	53	52	51	50	48	47	46	45	44	43	42
19	81	78	75	73	70	68	66	64	62	61	59	57	56	55	53	52	51	50	48	47	46	45	44
20	85	82	79	76	74	71	69	67	65	63	62	60	58	57	56	54	53	52	51	50	48	47	46
21	88	85	82	80	77	75	72	70	68	66	64	63	61	60	58	57	55	54	53	52	51	50	48
22	92	89	86	83	80	78	75	73	71	69	67	65	64	62	60	59	58	56	55	54	53	52	51
23	96	92	89	86	83	81	78	76	74	72	70	68	66	65	63	61	60	59	57	56	55	54	53

Number of years of contributions which count towards basic pension

	27	28	29	30	31	32	33	34	35	36	37	38	39	40	41	42	43	44	45	46	47	48	49
24	100	96	93	89	89	86	83	80	78	75	73	71	69	67	67	65	64	62	60	59	58	56	55
25	100	100	97	93	93	90	87	84	81	79	76	74	72	70	70	68	66	65	63	61	60	59	57
26	100	100	100	97	97	93	90	87	84	82	79	77	75	73	73	71	69	67	65	64	62	61	60
27	100	100	100	100	100	97	94	90	88	85	82	80	78	75	75	73	72	70	68	66	65	63	62
28		100	100	100	100	100	97	94	91	88	85	83	80	78	78	76	74	72	70	69	67	66	64
29			100	100	100	100	100	97	94	91	88	86	83	81	81	79	77	75	73	71	70	68	66
30				100	100	100	100	100	97	94	91	89	86	84	84	82	79	77	75	74	72	70	69
31					100	100	100	100	100	97	94	92	89	87	87	84	82	80	78	76	74	73	71
32						100	100	100	100	100	97	95	92	89	89	87	85	83	80	79	77	75	73
33							100	100	100	100	100	98	95	92	92	90	87	85	83	81	79	77	75
34								100	100	100	100	100	98	95	95	92	90	88	85	83	81	80	78
35									100	100	100	100	100	98	98	95	93	90	88	86	84	82	80
36										100	100	100	100	100	100	98	95	93	90	88	86	84	82
37											100	100	100	100	100	100	98	95	93	91	89	87	85
38												100	100	100	100	100	100	98	95	93	91	89	87
39													100	100	100	100	100	100	98	96	93	91	89
40														100	100	100	100	100	100	98	96	94	91
41															100	100	100	100	100	100	98	96	94
42																100	100	100	100	100	100	98	96
43																	100	100	100	100	100	100	98
44																		100	100	100	100	100	100
45																			100	100	100	100	100
46																				100	100	100	100
47																					100	100	100
48																						100	100
49																							100

Source: Department of Social Security

Women born after 5 April 1950 but before 6 March 1955 have a working life of 45, 46, 47 or 48 years depending on their state pension age (see p.40). At the time of writing, the government could not say how many qualifying years these women would need in order to obtain a given level of pension, but Chart 3.2 on pages 48–49 is likely to be a reasonable guide.

Use Chart 3.1 to work out the length of your working life.

EXAMPLE 3.3

Peggy was born in 1939 and is now 55. Her working life runs from the tax year in which she reached age 16 to the last tax year before she'll reach age 60 – 44 years in total. So far, Peggy has 28 qualifying years, built up before she married and since going back to work when her children started secondary school. This would entitle her to a basic pension of just under three-quarters (72 per cent) of the full rate – in other words, £41.47 a week at the 1994–95 pension rate. If she carries on making contributions until pension age, she'll build up 32 qualifying years which will entitle her to a pension of 83 per cent of the full rate – £47.81 at the 1994–95 pension rate.

If you are older

The present system of basic pensions started on 5 July 1948. If you were already 16 on that date, the system could work unfairly if your working life were deemed to have started at that age. Therefore, special rules exist which can protect your pension position if you were born before 5 July 1932. They work by reducing the length of your working life and, thus, the number of years of contributions which you need in order to qualify for a given level of basic pension. Chart 3.1 earlier shows how the rules affect you.

Chart 3.2 on pages 48 and 49 shows the percentage of the full rate of basic pension that you're entitled to, given the length of your working life and the number of qualifying contribution years that you have.

EXAMPLE 3.4

Leonard was born on 7 September 1929. He wasn't working on 5 July 1948, so his working life started on 6 April 1948 and ran until 5 April 1994 – a total of 46 years, instead of the usual 49 years for a man. Leonard needed only 41 years of contributions in order to qualify for a full basic pension instead of the usual 44 years.

Unfortunately, a few people – mainly women who married and stopped work before July 1948 – lose out under the rules because National Insurance they paid before they were married falls outside the definition of their working life and no longer counts towards their pension.

CHAPTER 4

STATE EARNINGS RELATED PENSION

The State Earnings Related Pension Scheme (SERPS)

How much pension?

STATE **Earnings Related Pension Scheme (SERPS)** pensions are additional state pensions which many people build up through paying Class 1 National Insurance. As the name suggests, SERPS pensions are linked to your earnings and so the amount received varies from person to person.

Your SERPS pension is worked out using a complicated formula. Thankfully, you don't need to be able to work it out for yourself, as the DSS will provide you with a statement of your SERPS entitlement (see p.56). For those who'd like to know more about how SERPS pensions are calculated, the appendix to this chapter gives details. Here, we give just a broad outline.

SERPS pensions are based on your earnings. Not all earnings are taken into account – only those over the lower earnings limit (see p.32) and up to an **upper earnings limit**. The upper earnings limit is set by the government each year and is £430 a week for the 1994–95 tax year. The pension is based on an average of these earnings over your whole working life, or your working life since 6 April 1978 if you reached age 16 before the date (but see the appendix if you'll reach state pension age before 6 April 1999). The amount of pension you qualify for is increased in line with earnings inflation up to the time you reach state pension age, and increases in line with price inflation once it's being paid.

If your earnings are equal to or above the upper earnings limit throughout your whole working life, you'll qualify for the maximum SERPS pension possible. Table 4.1 below gives a rough guide to the maximum SERPS pension you might get in today's money, and is based on the 1994–95 earning limits. The amount varies according to when you reach state pension age largely because of changes that have been made to the SERPS system. If your earnings are at any time lower than the upper earnings limit, or you didn't belong to SERPS for part of your working life, your SERPS pension will be smaller than the amounts shown in the table. SERPS pensions can be any amount from nothing up to the maximum shown in the table.

Government figures show that, in fact, most people's SERPS pensions fall far short of the maximum possible: in September 1992, the average state pension, including SERPS, based on their own contribution records, was £66.13 for men and £53.13 for women.

Table 4.1: Guide to the maximum SERPS pension you could have (in today's money)

If you reach state pension age in the tax year:	The maximum SERPS pension in 1994–95 £££ [1]	
	£ a week	£ a year
1994–95	82	4,264
2000–01	109	5,668
2005–06	99	5,148
2010–11	90	4,680
2020–21	86	4,472
2030–31	82	4,264
2040–41 and after	74	3,848

[1] The table assumes that you're a member of SERPS for as many years as possible and have earnings equal to, or above, the upper earnings limit (£22,360 in 1994–95)

EXAMPLE 4.1

Jonathan started work in 1966 and joined SERPS when it started in 1978. He'll reach the state pension age of 65 in 2010. If he was in SERPS for the whole of that time, and earned at least as much as the upper earnings limit each year, he'd qualify for a SERPS pension of £4,680 a year, in today's money. In fact, he's earned consistently less than the upper earnings limit and looks likely to have an eventual SERPS pension of only half that amount.

Who qualifies?

You can be in SERPS only if you count as an employee; you're not in SERPS during any periods when you're self-employed. In some circumstances, you can belong to SERPS, but not build up SERPS pension; during these periods, your earnings for SERPS purposes count as zero. Since, for anyone retiring from 6 April 1999 onwards, the SERPS pension is based on earnings in *all* the years in his or her working life (or since 6 April 1978), periods of zero earnings will reduce the eventual pension. Even for people retiring before 6 April 1999, whose SERPS pension is based on their best 20 years' earnings (or as many years' earnings as they have built up since 1978), the pension still builds up over their whole working life since 6 April 1978, so gaps in their SERPS membership (for example, due to periods of self-employment or because earnings for SERPS purposes count as zero) will result in a scaling down of the pension.

You'll be deemed to have zero earnings for SERPS purposes in the following situations:

- if you're low-paid. If you earn less than the lower earnings limit (£57 per week in the 1994–95 tax year – see p.32). You pay no National Insurance and build up neither basic nor SERPS pension
- if you're a married woman paying National Insurance at the married woman's reduced rate (see Chapter 12)
- if you're paying voluntary Class 3 National Insurance (see p.34). These count only towards the state basic pension, not SERPS
- if you're unemployed. Though you get National Insurance credits (see p.33), these count only towards the basic pension, not SERPS.

If you stay at home to care for children, or for a sick or elderly relative, you may qualify for Home Responsibilities Protection (see p.33). For anyone reaching state pension age on or after 6 April 1999, though you won't build up any SERPS pension while you qualify for Home Responsibilities Protection, these periods are not counted in your SERPS record at all and can't reduce the pension that you eventually get. Your SERPS record is protected in a similar way, if you're getting National Insurance credits because you're incapable of work – because you are ill or disabled, for example. But, in either of these cases, the part of your working life which counts towards SERPS can't be reduced to fewer than 20 years. These measures don't apply to people reaching state pension age before 6 April 1999.

When is SERPS paid?

SERPS pension can be paid once you reach the state pension age – 65 for men and 60 for women, at present, but increasing to 65 by 2020 (see p.40). If you put off starting to receive your state basic pension (see p.36), you'll also have to put off taking your SERPS pension. The deferred SERPS pension will be increased by 7.5 per cent for each year, in the same way as the deferred basic pension. The longest time you can put off starting to take your pension is five years – SERPS pensions, as well as basic pensions, are automatically paid once you reach age 65 if you're a woman, or 70 if you're a man. Following equalisation of the state pension ages for men and women, you'll be able to defer your SERPS pension, along with the basic pension, indefinitely and 'earn' an extra 10 per cent pension increase for each year you do this (see p.41).

Graduated pensions

There was an old state earnings related pension scheme, which ran from 6 April 1961 to 5 April 1975 and provided **graduated pensions**. If you belonged to the scheme, the National Insurance you paid was related to your earnings. The total that you paid is divided into units: if you're a woman, every £9 you paid counts as one unit; if you're a man, every £7.50 that you paid counts as a unit.

How much pension you get depends on how many units you have. In the 1994–95 tax year, each unit is worth 7.48 pence a week. This means that the biggest graduated pension a man could have is £6.43 a week. The biggest graduated pension a woman could have is £5.38. Though graduated pensions are now increased each year in line with price inflation, they will never be large pensions. The scheme wasn't designed to cope with the very high rates of inflation that Britain experienced during the 1970s; the buying power of graduated pensions was badly eroded during that time and there's no mechanism for allowing it to catch up.

As with the SERPS scheme, you may have been contracted out of the graduated pension scheme, which meant that your employer took over the responsibility of ensuring that you were paid an equivalent amount of pension at retirement – called the **Equivalent Pension Benefit** or EPB.

More information

Your main source of help and information about SERPS and graduated pensions is the Department of Social Security (DSS) – see p.41. It produces the following leaflets which may be helpful when looking at earnings-related pension entitlements:

Table 4.2: State Earnings Related Pension: useful DSS leaflets

NP46	A guide to state retirement pensions
CF411	Home Responsibilities Protection

You can get a statement of your current SERPS (and other state pensions) entitlement and a forecast of what it could be by retirement by contacting the Retirement Pension Forecast and Advice (RPFA) service – see p.42. The service will provide details of any graduated pension you qualify for as well. Complete Form BR19 (from DSS offices) and return it to the address on the form. Note that DSS forecasts are not made on the same basis as forecasts for personal pension plans (see p.197–98), so you can't compare them.

APPENDIX TO CHAPTER 4

How to work out your SERPS pension

You don't need to work out your SERPS pension for yourself – the DSS will do that for you. To do the calculations yourself requires some numerical skills and a certain amount of foraging for figures. You are not recommended to try to calculate the figures for yourself. If, however, you wish to know more about the way in which SERPS pensions are calculated, here is an outline.

Step 1 For each year since April 1978, earnings on which you've paid Class 1 contributions at the full rate are taken. This will be all your earnings if you earn less than the upper earnings limit, or your earnings up to that limit if you earn more. (Any earnings above the upper earnings limit are ignored.) The upper earnings limits for each year are shown in Table 4.3 overleaf.

Step 2 Each tax year's earnings are increased in line with changes in national average earnings – these are called your **revalued earnings**.

Step 3 The lower earnings limit for the last full tax year before the year in which you retire is subtracted from each year's revalued earnings. What's left is called your **surplus earnings**.

Step 4 Your SERPS pension is a fraction of your surplus earnings. The fraction, or fractions, used depends on when you retire:

Table 4.3: Upper earnings limits since April 1978

Tax year	Weekly limit	Monthly equivalent	Yearly equivalent
1978–79	£120	£520.00	£ 6,240.00
1979–80	£135	£585.00	£ 7,020.00
1980–81	£165	£715.00	£ 8,580.00
1981–82	£200	£866.67	£10,400.04
1982–83	£220	£953.33	£11,439.96
1983–84	£235	£1,018.33	£12,219.96
1984–85	£250	£1,083.33	£12,999.96
1985–86	£265	£1,148.33	£13,779.96
1986–87	£285	£1,235.00	£14,820.00
1987–88	£295	£1,279.00	£15,340.00
1988–89	£305	£1,322.00	£15,860.00
1989–90	£325	£1,409.00	£16,900.00
1990–91	£350	£1,517.00	£18,200.00
1991–92	£390	£1,690.00	£20,280.00
1992–93	£405	£1,755.00	£21,060.00
1993–94	£420	£1,820.00	£21,840.00
1994–95	£430	£1,864.00	£22,360.00

- if you retire on or before 5 April 1999, you get one-eightieth of each year's surplus earnings (up to a maximum of 20 years). This means that the biggest SERPS pension you can have is a quarter (20 × ¹⁄₈₀) of your average surplus earnings
- if you retire after 5 April 1999, the fraction is gradually reduced until, eventually, the biggest SERPS pension will be one-fifth of your average surplus earnings.

Chart 4.1 on pp.60 and 61 summarises the four steps.

EXAMPLE 4.2

Alfred retires in May 1994, aged 65. He's been in SERPS since 6 April 1984. His SERPS pension was worked out as follows:

Step 1 His earnings for each year are shown in column 1 of the table opposite. In most of the years, they were below the upper earnings limits and so the full amounts counted towards SERPS.

But, in 1988–89 and 1989–90, Alfred's earnings exceeded the upper limit and the excess amounts do not count – instead, the upper earnings limits for those years are used in the calculation. (The relevant figures are shown underlined in columns 2 and 3.)

Step 2 Alfred's earnings are revalued in line with average earnings up to the last complete tax year (1993–94) before he reaches the state pension age of 65. This gives revalued earnings as shown in column 5 of the table.

Step 3 The lower earnings limit, a yearly amount of £2,912 in 1993–94, is deducted from each revalued earnings figure to leave the surplus earnings shown in column 6 of the table.

Step 4 Adding together surplus earnings, as shown in column 6, comes to £188,556. One-eightieth of this total is £2,357. In other words, Alfred is entitled to a SERPS pension of £45.33 a week. This is increased each year in line with changes in the Retail Prices Index.

Table 4.4

1 Year	2 Alfred's earnings £	3 Upper earnings limit £	4 Revaluation factor [1] %	5 Revalued earnings £	6 Surplus earnings £
1984–85	11,000	13,000[2]	97.6	21,736	18,824
1985–86	11,700	13,780[2]	85.4	21,692	18,780
1986–87	13,500	14,820	70.3	22,991	20,079
1987–88	14,650	15,340	58.6	23,235	20,323
1988–89	16,230	15,860	45.8	23,124	20,212
1989–90	17,400	16,900	32.1	22,325	19,413
1990–91	18,100	18,200	23.1	22,281	19,369
1991–92	19,000	20,280	11.8	21,242	18,330
1992–93	19,000	21,060	5.0	19,950	17,038
1993–94	19,100	21,840	–	19,100	16,188
					188,556

[1] As published in the *Revaluation of Earnings Factors Order* 1993
[2] Rounded to the nearest £

Chart 4.1: How your SERPS pension is worked out

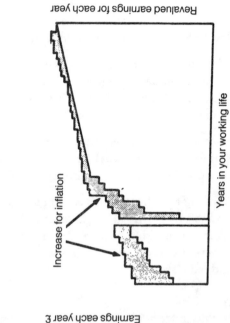

Revalued earnings for each year

Increase for inflation

Years in your working life

Step 2: Revalued earnings

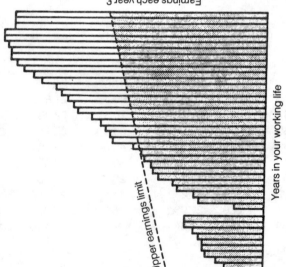

Earnings each year £

Upper earnings limit

Years in your working life

Step 1: Your earnings

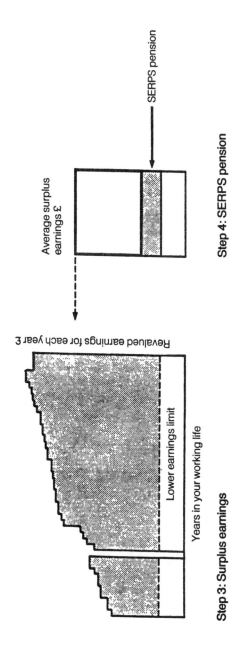

SERPS pension

Average surplus earnings £

Step 4: SERPS pension

Revalued earnings for each year £

Lower earnings limit

Years in your working life

Step 3: Surplus earnings

CHAPTER 5

EMPLOYER PENSION SCHEMES

MANY employers set up and run schemes which are designed to provide retirement pensions for their employees, and often other benefits as well, such as life insurance and pensions for widows and children. Employer schemes are attractive ways of saving for retirement because your employer pays in money on your behalf, and most qualify for the following tax reliefs:

- you and your employer both get tax relief on contributions to the scheme
- the invested contributions build up tax-free
- part of the proceeds can usually be taken as a tax-free lump sum at retirement.

Who qualifies?

A scheme may be open to all employees, or restricted to employees in a particular group – for example, there might be one scheme for works staff and another for management.

If your employer runs a scheme for which you are eligible, you don't have to join it; and, if you're already a member, you can leave the scheme. But there may be restrictions on joining or rejoining the scheme later on, for example, it might not accept employees over a certain age, or it might not be open to employees who were previously members but had chosen to leave.

Not all employers have a pension scheme. If you're not covered by an employer scheme, you should look into making your own pension arrangements (see Chapter 6).

How much pension?

How much pension you build up depends in part on the type of scheme you belong to. There are two main types of employer pension schemes: **final pay schemes** (also called **final salary schemes**, these are the most common type of **defined benefit scheme**) and **money purchase schemes** (**defined contribution schemes**).

Final pay schemes

The majority of people in an employer pension scheme belong to this type of scheme. The pension you get depends on your pay at, or near, retirement and the number of years that you've been in the scheme. For example, you might get one-eightieth or one-sixtieth of your pre-retirement pay for each year in the scheme. The major advantages of final pay schemes are that your pension entitlement generally keeps pace with changes in your earnings while you are working, and you have a good idea of how much pension you'll get in terms of your earnings just before retirement. This gives you a guide to the standard of living you can afford in retirement and helps you to work out if you're saving enough. But final pay schemes can be unattractive if you expect to change jobs before retirement (see Chapter 8), though there have been major improvements in this area.

'Final pay' will be defined in the scheme's rules. It can have a variety of meanings – for example, pay at a specified date, your average pay over the last three years, the best three years' pay out of the last ten, and so on.

'Pay' may mean just your basic salary, or it might be defined to include overtime pay, bonuses, commission, and so on. Some schemes adjust the pension they'll pay you to take account of the basic pension you can get from the state. In this case, 'pay' may be your earnings less a slice equal to the amount of the state basic pension, or some multiple of it.

EXAMPLE 5.1

The stockbroking firm that Megan works for runs a final pay pension scheme. Megan has been a member for only a year so far, but if she makes a career with the firm until the normal retirement age of 65, she'll have 40 years' membership. The scheme pays a pension of one-sixtieth of final pay for each year, so she could qualify for a pension equal to two-thirds of her pre-retirement earnings (40 × $\frac{1}{60}$ × final pay).

Money purchase schemes

With these, your pension depends on the amount you and your employer contribute, how well the invested contributions grow, and how much pension the investment will 'buy' when you reach retirement (called the **annuity rate**). Unlike final pay schemes, there's no automatic link between your pay and your pension, and you can't so easily estimate in advance how much pension you'll get. This makes retirement planning a bit more difficult. But, with this type of scheme, your expected pension isn't necessarily affected by job changes (see Chapter 8).

EXAMPLE 5.2

Angela is 46 and earns £10,000 a year working for a small travel agency. It runs a money purchase scheme for its staff. Angela pays in five per cent of her pay, and the company pays in an amount equal to about eight per cent of her pay. The bulk of these contributions is invested to build up a cash fund which will be used at retirement to provide Angela with a pension. At this stage, it's impossible to say how much pension she'll get, but if she stayed with the company until retirement, and if the invested contributions grew at a modest rate of, say, one per cent a year more than price inflation, her cash fund might provide her with a pension at retirement of £2,600 a year in today's prices (assuming the annuity rate of 9 per cent for a woman aged 65 that was generally available at the time of writing) – less if the pension were guaranteed to increase throughout her retirement.

Hybrid schemes

Some employers run pension schemes which combine final pay and money purchase elements. For example, the scheme may usually pay out a money purchase pension but also guarantee that the amount won't be less than a pension worked out according to a final pay formula. Another scheme might usually pay out final pay pensions but guarantee that you'll get the full value of a notional cash fund worked out according to money purchase principles. Hybrid schemes attempt to combine the best of both worlds by providing pensions which tend to keep pace with earnings and which need not be affected by job moves.

EXAMPLE 5.3

Jonathan is a magazine journalist. His employer runs a 'hybrid' pension scheme. Jonathan and his employer each put an amount equal to five per cent of his salary into a pension fund which will provide a cash sum at retirement to 'buy' Jonathan's pension – in other words, this is a money purchase arrangement. But, Jonathan's employer also pays an amount – currently equal to three per cent of the salary bill – into the scheme which provides a sort of safety net. This enables the employer to guarantee that Jonathan's pension will not be less than one-hundredth of his final pay for each year of membership of the scheme.

Other types of scheme

There are a number of other less common types of pension scheme, which generally provide poorer pensions than final pay or money purchase schemes. These include:

- **average pay schemes** These work like final pay schemes, except that your pension is based on pay throughout your working life, rather than pay near retirement. In a good scheme, pay from the earlier years will have been adjusted to take account of inflation before your pension is worked out. (An average pay scheme which revalues pay from the earlier years can be even better than a final pay scheme for someone whose earnings peak in the middle of his or her working life)

- **salary grade schemes**   You 'earn' a set amount of pension for each year that your pay is within a specified band of earnings. The higher the earnings band, the greater the amount of pension
- **flat rate schemes**   You get a fixed amount of pension for each year that you're in the scheme.

Tax-free cash at retirement

Some schemes – especially those covering people who work for the public sector, for example, civil servants, teachers, local government staff – automatically provide a cash lump sum at retirement as well as a pension. With other schemes, you can choose to swap part of your pension for a lump sum. (Note that you must make this choice *at the time you retire*; you can't make it after your pension has started to be paid.)

Obviously, swapping pension for a lump sum means that your remaining pension will be smaller. How much smaller depends on your particular scheme. For example, a woman retiring at age 60 might give up £1 a year pension for each £11 of lump sum, while a man aged 65 might give up £1 of pension for each £9 of lump sum. The different 'trade-off' between pension and lump sum reflects the higher expected cost of providing the woman with a pension given the lower retirement age and higher life expectancy.

Usually, taking the lump sum is a good idea because it's completely tax-free, whereas the pension is taxed as income in the normal way. If taking a lump sum would reduce your pension to less than you need, it's often still worth taking it, but then using it to invest in a **purchased life annuity** from an insurance company. A purchased life annuity provides you with an income for life in exchange for a lump sum. Once you've made the investment you can't get your money back as a lump sum, but part of each annuity payment is treated as the return of your original investment. This part is tax-free; only the remaining income is taxable. This means you pay less tax on the total annuity 'income' than you'd pay on the same amount in pension from your pension scheme.

EXAMPLE 5.4

Iain is about to retire at age 65 and is entitled to a pension of £9,200 a year from his employer pension scheme. But Iain can take up to £20,700 as a tax-free lump sum. If he does this, his pension will be reduced to £6,900 a year. Iain also qualifies for a state basic pension of £2,995 in the 1994–95 tax year so, if he didn't take the lump sum, he'd have a total before-tax income of £12,195. After tax, this would be £10,346.

Suppose, instead, that Iain took the full lump sum and that he could use it to buy a purchased life annuity which would provide him with a before-tax income of £2,300 a year – just enough to keep his before-tax income at the same level of £12,195 (£2,995 + £6,900 + £2,300). After tax, this would be £10,744 – higher than in the 'pre-lump sum situation' because part of each annuity payment is not taxed as income but treated as (tax-free) return of capital.

In some situations, you should be wary of giving up your pension for a lump sum. For example, some employer schemes (mainly in the public sector) provide pensions which are guaranteed to increase in line with inflation. Others don't guarantee to do this, but have a track record of paying good increases. Guaranteed increases are usually taken into account in working out the lump sum, but non-guaranteed increases may not be. If income is your priority, it's not worth giving up these pensions to buy a purchased life annuity instead – you're unlikely to get as good a deal from the annuity as you can from the employer scheme. In most schemes, taking a lump sum reduces your own pension, but not any pensions for widows or children (see Chapter 9). If your health is poor, it may be a good idea to take the biggest lump sum that you can at the time you retire.

Inland Revenue limits

Employer pension schemes benefit from significant tax advantages, and so the Inland Revenue puts some limits on the amount of pension, and other benefits, that such schemes can provide. The main limits are set out in Table 5.1. They are set in relation to final pay and, in all but a few cases, these overall limits apply even to schemes which don't work out benefits in terms of final pay – in other words, the limits apply to money purchase schemes, flat rate schemes, salary grade schemes and so on, as well as final pay schemes. 'Final pay' for the purpose of these overall limits is defined in the tax legislation and is usually:

- your earnings in any one year out of the last five years before retirement
- the yearly average of your earnings during a three-year period ending any time within the last ten years before retirement. This is the more commonly used limit, and the one which must usually be used if you're a director of your own company.

Remember that these are Inland Revenue definitions – your employer scheme may use less generous definitions.

If your employer scheme is unusually generous, or if the Inland Revenue definition of final pay results in your pension benefits being limited to less than the available investment fund could 'buy', the earnings used to calculate final pay can be increased, up to retirement, in line with the relevant change in the Retail Prices Index. This process, **dynamisation**, effectively raises the Inland Revenue limits on all your benefits.

Normally, the maximum pension and other benefits build up over a period of 40 years: pension builds up at a rate of one-sixtieth of final pay for each year you're with the employer; the maximum lump sum builds up at a rate of three-eightieths of final pay for each year. If you can't build up your pension over such a long period as 40 years, the rules allow for a faster build up of pension. This can be especially useful for executives and high-fliers who – or whose employers – want to boost their pensions late on in working life. There are different rules, according to which pension regime applies.

Table 5.1: Main tax limits on your pension from an employer scheme

Description of scheme to which you currently belong [1]	Limit on your pension [2] at retirement [3]	Limit on your lump sum at retirement [3]
'Post-1989 regime' a) Scheme set up on or after 14 March 1989, or b) Scheme set up before 14 March 1989 but you joined on or after 1 June 1989, or c) Scheme set up before 14 March 1989 which you joined on or after 17 March 1987 but before 1 June 1989, if you elect to be treated under the 'post-1989 regime'	Two-thirds of final pay up to a maximum of £51,200 [4]	One-and-a-half times final pay up to a maximum of £115,200 [4]
'1987–89 regime' Scheme set up before 14 March 1989 which you joined on or after 17 March 1987 and before 1 June 1989 (unless you opted to be treated under the 'post-1989 regime' – see above)	Two-thirds of final pay	One-and-a-half times final pay up to a maximum of £150,000
'Pre-1987 regime' Scheme you joined before 17 March 1987	Two-thirds of final pay	One-and-a-half times final pay

[1] As well as the three categories of scheme listed here, it is possible for you to have joined a scheme after 1987 or 1989 but for pre-1987 or pre-1989 rules to apply, for example, where your employer's business has been restructured or merged with another business, or where you changed from one of your employer pension schemes to another due to promotion

[2] This is the limit which applies if all your benefits from the scheme are taken as pension. If part is taken as a lump sum (or certain other benefits), the maximum you can take as pension is reduced to less than the amounts shown in this column

[3] Under the '1987–89 regime' and 'pre-1987 regime', these maximum limits apply at the normal retirement date for the scheme. Under the 'post-1989 regime', the limits apply at any age within the range 60 to 75

[4] This is the limit proposed for the 1994–95 tax year. The limit is based on an 'earnings cap' which puts a ceiling on the amount of final pay which can be used in the calculation. The earnings cap is usually increased each year in line with the Retail Prices Index and is set at £76,800 for 1994–95, if the November 1993 Budget measures pass into law

Under the 'pre–1987 regime', you usually need to have belonged to the scheme for at least ten years by the time you reach retirement in order to qualify for a full two-thirds maximum pension. The maximum possible lump sum is reached after 20 years. The maximum rates of pension and lump sum build up are shown in Table 5.2.

Table 5.2: Maximum pension and lump sum build up under the 'pre-1987 regime'

Years of service	Pension as a fraction of final pay	Lump sum as a fraction of final pay
1	1/60	3/80
2	2/60	6/80
3	3/60	9/80
4	4/60	12/80
5	5/60	15/80
6	8/60	18/80
7	16/60	21/80
8	24/60	24/80
9	32/60	30/80
10	40/60	36/80
11		42/80
12		48/80
13		54/80
14		63/80
15		72/80
16		81/80
17		90/80
18		99/80
19		108/80
20		120/80

Under the '1987–89 regime', you must have at least 20 years' membership, by retirement, in order to qualify for the maximum two-thirds pension. The fastest rate at which the pension can build up is one-thirtieth of final pay for each year. You need at least 20 years' service up to retirement to qualify for the maximum lump sum. The rules regarding the maximum rate at which a lump sum builds up are complicated – broadly, the proportion by which the lump sum has been boosted must match the proportion by which the related maximum pension has been boosted – see example 5.5.

If you are covered by the 'post-1989 regime', the lump sum must not exceed 2¼ times the maximum pension (before any has been swapped for a lump sum). Whichever regime applies, the lump sum must not exceed 1½ times final pay and must comply with the cash limits described in Table 5.1 on p.69.

EXAMPLE 5.5

Chris became a manager with a finanace company on 18 March 1987, and joined the pension scheme from that date. Suppose he stays until he reached 65, by which time he has 20 years' service. By then, his final pay will be £60,000 (in today's money). The pension scheme is a generous one which will allow him to take a larger pension than a straight 'sixtieths' formula would allow. If the scheme did pay just one-sixtieth of his final pay for each year of membership, he would qualify for a pension of $\frac{1}{60}$ × 20 × £60,000 = £20,000. The Inland Revenue rules allow a faster rate of pension build up, and the maximum pension allowed would be one-thirtieth of final pay for each year, up to a maximum pension of two-thirds of final pay. This gives a maximum possible pension under the rules of $\frac{2}{3}$ × £60,000 = £40,000.

The maximum boost – in the jargon, 'uplift' – to his pension is £40,000 − £20,000 = £20,000. In practice, the scheme is not quite so generous. It allows him to take a pension of £30,000. So the actual uplift is £10,000/£20,000 = ½ of the maximum uplift allowed by the tax rules.

If the lump sum he can take had built up according to the ordinary rules, the most he could have would be three-eightieths of his final pay for each year of service. This would come to $\frac{3}{80}$ × 20 × £60,000 = £45,000. But the tax rules allow him more than this: referring to the 'pre-March 1987 regime' table opposite, the maximum lump sum after 20 years' service would be 1½ times final pay – in other words £90,000. This would give a maximum possible uplift of £90,000 − £45,000 = £45,000. But his actual pension was boosted by only one-half of the maximum possible uplift. The tax rules require that his lum sum is boosted only by the same fraction. Thus, the maximum lump sum Chris can have is £45,000 + (½ × £45,000) = £67,500

Where the pension build-up rate exceeds one-sixtieth of final pay for each year of service, the maximum two-thirds-of-final-pay pension limit applies after taking account of any pensions you'll get from pension schemes and plans you've built up in the past – not just the pension from your current employer scheme. Similarly, if the lump sum builds up at a faster rate than three-eightieths of final pay per year, the limit applies after taking account of lump sums from other schemes and plans you have.

When is your employer pension paid?

Your employer scheme sets a normal pension age at which you will usually start to receive your pension. Until just a few years ago, it was common for schemes to set a lower pension age for women than for men, and the most favoured option was to choose the same ages as are currently used for the state pension – i.e. 60 for women and 65 for men. However, following a ruling by the European court (see p.166), it has been clear, for the last few years, that unequal pension ages cannot continue. In its annual survey of employer pension schemes, the National Association of Pension Funds (NAPF) found that nearly 85 per cent of the 852 schemes in the survey now have the same pension age for men and women. The most popular age was 65, chosen by 59 per cent of those schemes with an equal age; 28 per cent had equalised at age 60.

The tax rules prevent the maximum possible pensions being paid at very early ages. Under the 'pre-1987 regime' and the '1987–89 regime', the maximum pension can't usually be paid before age 60 (men) and 55 (women). For the 'post-1989 regime', the lowest age at which full pensions can be paid is 50. There are exceptions: for example, people in certain professions – such as divers or professional footballers – can retire earlier with a full pension. Special rules apply if you have to retire early due to ill health (see Chapter 10).

Pension increases

Once you start to receive your pension, it can be increased as long as it doesn't exceed the amount of the maximum possible pension allowed under the Inland Revenue rules (see Table 5.1) increased in line with changes in the Retail Prices Index.

Legislation has been passed that allows rules to be introduced requiring certain pensions to be at least partially protected against inflation. The rules – called limited price indexation, or LPI for short – would apply only to final pay schemes and would require pensions, which are built up after a date yet to be announced, to be increased in line with price inflation up to a maximum of five per cent a year once the pension starts to be paid. However, there has been a long delay in putting this legislation into effect and it looks as if the requirement may now be dropped.

Only a very limited version of LPI has been introduced so far. Where a pension scheme has more assets than are needed to fund the pensions and other benefits (i.e. it has a 'surplus'), it is required to use the surplus by providing LPI for all pensions built up before paying any of the surplus to the employer. This rule applies only to final pay schemes which have made payments to the employer on or after 17 August 1990.

In an ideal world, pensions would automatically increase in line with inflation – however high it happened to be – in order to protect the original buying power of the pension. In practice, few employers are willing to take on the open-ended commitment that such a promise represents. Commonly, the larger pension schemes offer a guaranteed increase up to a limited level – for example, in line with inflation up to a maximum of 3 per cent a year – but may make further discretionary increases if they can afford to. A recent survey by the journal *Occupational Pensions* found that out of 82 schemes 16 guarantee increases of around 3 per cent which might be topped up by discretionary increases; 44 schemes guarantee to increase pensions in line with inflation up to a ceiling – commonly 5 per cent a year – though some of these schemes pay discretionary increases too. Only eight schemes guaranteed to match inflation however high it turned out to be. Eleven schemes offered no *guaranteed* increases at all.

What do you pay?

Some employer schemes are **non-contributory**. This means that your employer pays the whole cost of the scheme and you contribute nothing. The majority of schemes, however, are **contributory**, which means that you pay part of the cost and your employer pays part. Usually, you pay a given proportion of your salary into the scheme, commonly around five per cent.

With money purchase schemes, your employer will also pay a specified amount or percentage of your salary. But with final pay schemes (and other defined benefit schemes), the employer will provide however much is needed to make up the balance of the cost of providing the pensions and other benefits.

Both you and your employer get tax relief on contributions to an employer scheme. Tax relief on your contributions is given by deducting them from your pay before your tax bill is worked out, and you get relief up to your highest rate of tax.

EXAMPLE 5.6

Megan earns £16,000 a year working for a stockbroking firm and is a member of the pension scheme. The firm pays most of the cost of the scheme, but Megan contributes three per cent of her pay, which comes to £480 a year. However, the cost to Megan is less than this because she gets tax relief on the contributions. As she pays tax at the basic rate of 25 per cent on at least £480 of her income, the after-tax-relief cost of the contributions is only £360. (You can work it out: £480 × [1−0.25] = £360.)

The Inland Revenue limits the amount you can contribute to an employer scheme. The limit is 15 per cent of your earnings. If you are covered by the 'pre-1987 regime' or the '1987–89 regime', there's no other limit on the amount you can contribute. But, if the 'post-1989 regime' applies to you, there's also an overall cash limit on the amount which can qualify for tax relief. The proposed limit for the 1994–95 tax year is £11,520. The cash limit is usually increased each year in line with inflation as measured by the Retail Prices Index. Table 5.3 below gives some examples of how much you can pay into an employer pension scheme, depending on the amount you earn. There's no Inland Revenue limit on the amount your employer can pay into a scheme as such, though there are rules to prevent him or her paying in more than is needed to provide the maximum possible benefits.

Table 5.3: The most you can pay into a pension scheme

Yearly earnings [1]	Maximum yearly contributions	After-tax-relief cost of contributions	
		25% taxpayer	40% taxpayer
£	£	£	£
10,000	1,500	1,125	900
15,000	2,250	1,688	1,350
20,000	3,000	2,250	1,800
25,000	3,750	2,813	2,250
30,000	4,500	3,375	2,700
40,000	6,000	[2]	3,600
50,000	7,500	[2]	4,500
60,000	9,000	[2]	5,400
70,000	10,500	[2]	6,300
80,000	12,000 [3]	[2]	7,200 [3]

[1] Including the taxable value of most fringe benefits
[2] Unlikely to be applicable
[3] If the 'post-1989 regime' applies to you (see Table 5.1 on p.69), the maximum contribution in the 1994–95 tax year is £11,520 (assuming the November 1993 Budget proposals become law), which would cost a 40 per cent taxpayer £6,912

Too little pension?

As long as your total contributions remain within the tax limits, you can make extra pension contributions in order to boost your eventual pension. You can also use extra contributions to boost other benefits, such as life cover and pensions for dependants (see Chapter 9) or increases to your pension once it's being paid. But extra contributions under an arrangement which you started on or after 17 March 1987 can't usually be used to provide or increase a tax-free lump sum.

Extra contributions are called **Additional Voluntary Contributions (AVCs)**. You can pay them either to an AVC scheme set up by your employer – all employer schemes must have an AVC facility if employees demand it – or to your own **free-standing AVC (FSAVC) scheme**, which is a scheme independent of your employer's pension arrangements.

Many employer AVC schemes, and all FSAVC schemes, work on a money purchase basis – in other words, your contributions are invested and build up a cash fund which is used at retirement to provide pension or other benefits. Some employers with final pay pension schemes have AVC schemes which work in a different way: your contributions are used to 'buy' extra years in the scheme. This has the effect of increasing your pension and any other benefits (including tax-free lump sums) which are based on your years of membership.

EXAMPLE 5.7

Peggy went back to work as a teacher after taking a number of years off to bring up her three children. She's belonged to the pension scheme for 16 years, and will have 21 years in the scheme by the time she reaches normal retirement age. In order to increase her eventual pension, Peggy is making AVCs into her employer scheme. These 'buy' her extra years of membership, so that by retirement she will be credited with 25 years' membership instead of 21. This will increase her pension by approximately £1,000 in today's money – the extra pension is guaranteed to increase in line with inflation once it's being paid.

You can't use AVCs to boost your pension or other benefits beyond the Inland Revenue limits (see p.68). In the past, if you'd paid more in AVCs than was needed to bring your pension and other benefits up to the maximum level, the 'excess AVCs' were wasted. For schemes set up from 27 July 1989 onwards, any excess AVCs can be repaid at retirement, after tax, at a special rate of 35 per cent, has been deducted. Schemes set up before 27 July 1989 can also repay excess AVCs, but can't be forced to do so. You can't reclaim tax deducted from a refund of AVCs, and if you're a higher rate taxpayer you'll be required to pay some extra tax on the refund (see p.222).

Executive schemes and small self-administered schemes

Executive schemes are special pension schemes designed for a small number of members – for example, an individual manager, or a group of directors. If you're a high-flier, your employer might operate such a scheme. They are also a possible choice if you run your own business as a company. Executive schemes are bound by the same rules as other employer schemes – so the benefit and contribution limits outlined in this chapter apply – but they work more like a personal plan: they are offered by investment and insurance companies who invest your contributions to build up a fund which will provide your pension benefits. The scheme provider charges you for administration and management of the investments.

Small self-administered schemes (SSASs) are small employer schemes – usually with fewer than 12 members and most often used to provide pensions, and other benefits, for high-fliers and/or executives within a company. They can be a good choice for family-run companies with sufficient resources. SSASs are administered by investment or insurance companies, actuaries or specialist benefit consultants. But the SSAS provider doesn't usually manage your investments itself. Instead, you have a wide choice about who will manage your money and how it will be invested. But this introduces an extra tier of management charges and makes these schemes unrealistic unless around £100,000 or more is available to invest. Like executive schemes, SSASs are bound by the normal rules for employer schemes, but the Inland Revenue also requires strict supervision of the membership and investments of an SSAS, including the appointment of a special trustee (see p.154).

In the past, SSASs have been popular with small businesses, particularly because they provided a route for investing in the business's own premises or other property and a means of making loans to the business. In March 1992, new laws came into effect which aim to stop all pension schemes and plans investing more than five per cent of their money in the employer's company – either in the company's property, or by way of loans. SSASs are exempt from this restriction as long as they meet certain conditions, for example, all members must also be trustees (see p.152) and all decisions about self-investment must be made by the trustees unanimously and in writing.

Top-up schemes

In general, very few employer schemes will promise or provide benefits which are anywhere near the maximum limits laid down by the Inland Revenue. However, the earnings cap which applies under the 'post-1989 regime' and sets an overall cash limit on the size of pension and lump sum you can get can be an unwelcome restriction on the pension benefits which a scheme can offer if you are a high earner.

In order to address this problem, at the time the earnings cap was introduced, the government also allowed for the establishment of top-up schemes which can be used to provide a pension (and other benefits) over and above the amounts allowed by the Inland Revenue limits. The drawback is that top-up schemes don't benefit from the special tax advantages which normallly apply to pension schemes, but, on the plus side, top-up schemes can be very flexible because you don't have to take the bulk of the pay-out as pension. There are two broad types of top-up scheme:

- **unfunded schemes** With these, your employer simply pays you benefits at the time you reach retirement. You are liable for income tax on the benefits (even if they are paid as a lump sum)
- **funded schemes** (also called Funded Unapproved Retirement Benefit Schemes of FURBS). Your employer pays contributions which build up a fund to provide the eventual benefits. At the time the contributions are made, they count as fringe benefits on which you're liable for income tax. Usually, the fund is arranged as a trust, and income and gains from the trust will generally be taxed only at the basic rate,

even if your own tax rate is higher than this. (The government has recently closed a loophole by which FURBS could be invested tax-free by using an offshore fund.) There is no tax to pay on the benefits when they are paid out.

From your point of view, a funded scheme offers better security because you know the money is being built up to pay the benefits. With an unfunded scheme, you could lose your top-up benefits if your employer went bust.

For 1994–95, the earnings cap is set at £76,800 – likely to be viewed by most people as a generous level – but the cap is increased periodically in line with *price* inflation, and for 1992–93 was not increased at all. Historically, prices have tended to rise on average by around 2 per cent less per year than earnings. This means that, although the earnings cap will usually rise each year, it will probably rise more slowly than actual earnings. On that basis, the earning cap will eventually limit the pensions of those on even quite modest salaries.

More information

If your employer runs a pension scheme which you are eligible to join, you must be given basic information about the scheme if you request it. Usually, this information will be in the form of an explanatory booklet which must be provided within one month of your request. The booklet will set out the type of scheme, the benefits it offers, whether or not it's contributory, who the scheme officials are and who to contact if you want to seek advice or make a complaint. Once you are a member of the scheme, you must be given this booklet within 13 weeks of joining. Read the booklet carefully and keep it in a safe place – it's your primary source of information about the scheme. You must be told about any changes to the basic information no later than one month after the change has occurred.

Scheme members and other beneficiaries (such as a member's wife or husband) have the right to information about their own particular benefits under the scheme. This is supplied in the form of a **benefit statement** which will tell you about the pension and lump sum you can expect at retirement, the amounts that would be payable if you died, and the benefits you'd have built up if you left the scheme. The scheme officials are, at present, not required to provide you automatically with benefit statements; you have the right to *request* a statement once a year, and the statement must be supplied within two months of your request. In practice, many schemes do automatically send employee members a statement regularly (usually once a year).

Members, other beneficiaries and your trade union all have the right to inspect the scheme documents, including the trust deed and rules. These are usually very technical documents which you'd only want to consult if you needed to check precisely how some aspect of the scheme worked. At present, you have the right to inspect the documents only once every twelve months. A reasonable charge can be made if you are supplied with copies of documents.

You also have the right to see the scheme's annual report and accounts and the report of the scheme actuary (usually made every three years). (The actuary estimates the size and timing of the benefits payable under the scheme and advises whether the assets in the fund are sufficient to meet the payments as they fall due.) Often, you'll receive a simplified report and accounts each year which give these details.

Your main source of additional information about your employer pension scheme is the scheme officials or your personnel department at work. The scheme officials are usually the pensions administrator and the trustees of the scheme. They are also the people you should go to initially if you have a problem. For more about what to do if you face problems concerning your employer scheme pension, see Chapter 15.

CHAPTER 6

PERSONAL PENSION PLANS

PERSONAL pension plans are a way of making your own pension arrangements by saving, usually with an insurance company, though unit trusts, building societies, banks or friendly societies are also allowed to offer pension plans. (Although banks and building societies do market plans, these are invariably run by life insurance companies either owned by the bank or society, or for whom the bank or society acts as an agent.) The organisation with which you save – here called the **plan provider** – invests your money to build up a cash fund. At retirement, the fund is used to provide your pension.

Personal pension plans can be used for contracting out of the State Earnings Related Pension Scheme (SERPS) – this aspect of the plans is dealt with in Chapter 7.

Who qualifies?

Anybody who is at least age 16 and under the age of 75 with earnings can take out a personal pension plan. You can't simultaneously belong to an employer pension scheme and pay into a personal pension plan, except in these cases:

- you have additional earnings from a source other than the employer who offers the pension scheme – for example, you may have income from private freelance or consultancy work
- the personal pension plan is used solely for 'contracting out' of SERPS – see Chapter 7
- the employer scheme provides *only* death benefits

● you are taxed on contributions made by your employer to the scheme on your behalf.

This means that many employees have to choose whether to be a member of their employer scheme or contribute to their own personal plan instead. A good employer scheme is hard to replace, so think carefully before opting for a personal plan.

Plan providers must contact you every five years if you are an employee and have taken out a regular premium plan (other than one used solely for contracting out of SERPS) to ensure that you are still eligible to have the plan. Make sure you reply to this enquiry, otherwise your plan may be stopped.

If you're self-employed, you have to make your own provision for retirement, and personal pension plans will generally be the best way of doing this (but see Chapter 16). If you run your own business as a company, a personal pension plan is one way in which you can save for retirement, but you might instead set up your own employer scheme (see pp.77–78).

Subject to the contribution limits (see p.88), you can generally contribute to more than one personal pension plan at a time.

How much pension?

All personal pension plans work on a **money purchase** basis (see p.64). This means that you can't, in advance, be sure of how much pension you'll get. The pension will depend on the amount you contribute, how the invested contributions grow, and the rate – **annuity rate** – at which your cash fund can be exchanged for pension at the time you retire. You have a choice about how your savings are invested – you'll find details in Chapter 13.

A personal plan can also provide benefits for your dependants, such as pensions for a widow or widower, or children (see Chapter 9). Using the plan to provide dependants' benefits reduces the amount to be used for your retirement pension. Similarly, you 'pay' extra (by receiving a lower pension at the start of your retirement) for a pension which increases after retirement – for example, by a fixed amount each year, or by enough to match inflation.

Tax-free cash at retirement

As with employer pension schemes, you can usually take part of the proceeds from a personal pension plan as a tax-free lump sum at retirement. Doing this obviously reduces the amount of pension you get, but, generally, taking the cash is worthwhile. If you can't manage on the reduced pension, you could use your tax-free cash to buy a **purchased life annuity**. As described on p.66, the after-tax income from a purchased life annuity is likely to exceed the after-tax amount of pension which you give up in order to take the tax-free cash. How much tax-free cash you can have depends on the type of personal plan that you have and when you first started it. The limits are shown in Table 6.1.

Table 6.1: How much tax-free cash you can have

Type of plan and when started	Maximum amount of tax-free cash
Old-style personal pension plans [1] (called retirement annuity contracts, section 620 plans or section 226 plans)	
Started before 17 March 1987	Three times the remaining pension
Started on or after 17 March 1987 and before 1 July 1988	Three times the remaining pension up to an overall maximum of £150,000 [2]
New-style personal pension plans [1]	
Started on or after 1 July 1988 and before 27 July 1989	One-quarter of pension fund (except amounts to be used to provide dependants' pensions) [3]
Started on or after 27 July 1989	One-quarter of pension fund (except amounts to be used to provide 'contracted-out' [4] pensions) without any overall maximum

[1] Old-style plans were available before 1 July 1988. Since then, only new-style plans have been allowed to be started. You can continue to save using an old-style plan if you have one
[2] The £150,000 limit applies to each plan (rather than per person). Thus, in practice, the effect of the limit could be avoided by taking out a cluster of several plans instead of just one
[3] Strictly speaking, a £150,000 overall cash limit per plan applies to lump sums taken from new-style plans started before 27 July 1989. In practice, the limit has no significance because, first, a cluster of plans could be arranged rather than a single plan and, secondly, the plan-holder can switch to another plan (which will not be subject to the cash limit) at retirement using the 'open market option' – see p.219.
[4] See Chapter 7

EXAMPLE 6.1

Geoff is about to retire. He has an old-style personal pension plan to which he has contributed for over 20 years. He can either take a pension from the plan of £9,300 a year, or take a lower pension and up to £21,000 as a tax-free lump sum. If he takes the maximum lump sum, his pension will be reduced to £7,000 a year.

EXAMPLE 6.2

Jack is saving for retirement using a new-style personal pension plan. If, by retirement, he builds up a fund of £143,000 (in terms of today's money), he could choose to take up to one-quarter of the fund – in other words, £35,750 – as a tax-free lump sum. If he did this, he'd be left with a pension of £12,850 a year instead of a full pension of £17,150 a year.

Pension increases

You decide whether to have a pension which is paid at a single flat rate or one which increases year by year at the time you want to start taking your pension. Most of the examples, so far, have – for the sake of simplicity – shown personal pensions (where applicable) which do not increase beyond their original level. However, in general, you would be wise to choose a pension which does include some built-in increases, even though this will reduce the starting level of the pension.

EXAMPLE 6.3

Samuel is 60 and ready to take things a bit easier. The time has come to convert the pool of investment which he has built up in one of his pension plans into pension, but first he must decide what sort of pension he wants. He can get a level pension of around £950 for every £10,000 he has built up in his plan.

Alternatively, every £10,000 could buy him a pension which starts at £600 but increases by five per cent each year.

If inflation averaged five per cent over the first ten years of his retirement, a level pension of £950 would be worth only £583 in terms of today's buying power, whereas the increasing pension would have kept its initial value of £600 in today's money.

Given that the future is uncertain – inflation may run at more or less than five per cent a year, and Samuel's retirement may be short or long – Samuel decides to opt for the relative security of the increasing pension despite the low starting level.

When is the pension paid?

You don't have to stop work in order to take a pension from a personal plan. However, the Inland Revenue lays down rules which prevent you taking your pension too early in life. With old-style personal plans – plans taken out before 1 July 1988 – you normally can't start to take your pension before you reach age 60. There are some exceptions – for example, if you have to retire through ill-health (see Chapter 10), or if you have an occupation for which an earlier retirement age has been officially recognised (see Table 6.2 overleaf).

With new-style personal plans – those taken out on or after 1 July 1988 – the rules allow you to take your pension from age 50 onwards, so for many of the occupations listed in Table 6.2, there's no need for special treatment. But the special retirement ages of 35, 40 and 45 apply to the occupations as shown in the case of new-style, as well as old-style, plans.

Inland Revenue rules prohibit you from paying into either a new-style or an old-style personal pension plan after reaching age 75, and that is the latest age at which you can start to draw your pension. Within the Inland Revenue age limits, the organisation providing the plan may have its own rules about the normal pension age. It's rare that a plan has a single fixed pension age. With some plans, you choose your own retirement age at the time you first take out the plan, though you may be able to change your mind later on. Other plans are even more flexible, and let you leave your decision until you're ready to start taking the pension. You can increase your scope for flexibility by having several pension plans and starting your pension from each at a different age. For example, you might have four plans with pension ages of 60, 61, 62 and 65. Having some flexibility is important because annuity rates may be low at the time you would have liked to start taking a pension. Since the level of annuity rates then affects the pension you get throughout your whole retirement, it would be better to put off starting your pension until rates have risen again.

Table 6.2: Occupations with early retirement ages

Age	Occupation	Age	Occupation
35	Athletes	45	Non-commissioned Royal
	Badminton players		Marine Reservists
	Boxers		
	Cyclists	50	Croupiers
	Dancers		Martial arts instructors
	Footballers		Money broker dealers
	Models		Newscasters
	National Hunt jockeys		Offshore riggers
	Rugby League players		Royal Navy Reservists
	Squash players		Rugby League referees
	Table tennis players		Territorial Army members
	Tennis players		
	Wrestlers	55	Air pilots
			Brass instrumentalists
40	Cricketers		Distant water trawlermen
	Golfers		In-shore fishermen
	Motor cycle riders		Money broker dealer
	Motor racing drivers		directors
	Speedway riders		National Health Service
	Trapeze artists		psychiatrists
	Divers		Nurses, midwives, etc.
			Part-time firemen
45	Flat-racing jockeys		Singers

The later you start taking your pension, the longer your pension fund is left invested and, usually, the longer you carry on making contributions. Since you'll be older when the pension starts (and your life expectancy will be lower – see p.10), the pension provider can expect to pay out the pension for a shorter period. This means that your pension is likely to be greater the later you start receiving it. Conversely, if you retire early, you'll generally have to make do with a smaller pension.

What do you pay?

You can choose whether to take out a plan (sometimes called a **regular premium** plan) which requires regular payments – for example, monthly or yearly – or a plan which requires only a single lump sum contribution (sometimes called a **single premium** pension plan). There may be a minimum contribution – for example, £20 a month or £200 a year with a regular payment plan, or £1,000 with a lump sum plan.

Most regular payment plans let you increase your contributions – either by a fixed amount each year, or in line with price or earnings inflation. Increases may be automatic, or optional. Generally, you should consider increasing your payments regularly, so that your pension savings don't fall back in terms of today's money. You may also be able to make extra one-off payments to your regular payment plan.

Many regular payment plans also allow you to reduce your payments, or miss a limited number of payments without penalty – though you may have to pay extra for this option. Chapter 13 looks, among other things, at the pros and cons of regular payment plans versus lump sum plans.

Tax relief on your savings

You get tax relief up to your highest rate of income tax on the amount you contribute to a personal pension plan. This means, for example, that a taxpayer paying tax at a 25 per cent rate can contribute £100 to a plan at a cost of only £75. The cost to a 40 per cent taxpayer of contributing £100 would be only £60 after tax relief.

With new-style personal plans (plans taken out on or after 1 July 1988), if you work for an employer you get basic rate tax relief automatically by paying only the after-tax-relief amount into your plan. The lower 20 per cent rate of income tax is ignored, so you'll get tax relief at the full basic rate even if you paid only 20 per cent tax on all, or part, of the income you're now paying into your plan. If you're a higher rate taxpayer, you have to claim the extra tax relief due. If you're self-employed, you make full before-tax-relief payments to your plan provider and must claim through your tax office the tax relief due to you.

With old-style pension plans (those taken out before 1 July 1988), all payments are made before taking account of tax relief. You have to claim the tax relief due to you. You can make a claim for tax relief on your personal pension contributions either through your Tax Return, or by using Form PP120 which you can get from your tax office.

EXAMPLE 6.4

Ryan is 45 and finance director of a small knitwear firm. In the 1994–95 tax year he contributes £8,500 (before tax relief) to his new-style personal pension plan. He receives basic-rate tax relief of £2,125 (25 per cent of £8,500) automatically, by handing over just £6,375 to the insurance company which runs his plan. But Ryan pays higher-rate tax of 40 per cent on at least £8,500 of his income, so he can claim additional tax relief of £1,275 (40 per cent of £8,500 less the basic-rate tax relief already given). The total after-tax-relief cost to him of the £8,500 contribution is only £5,100 (£8,500 less basic rate relief of £2,125 and less higher rate relief of £1,275).

Limits on what you pay

The Inland Revenue limits the amount of pension contributions you can make which will qualify for tax relief. The limits vary according to your age and the type of personal plan. They are set as a percentage of your **net relevant earnings**. If you're an employee, this means your total before-tax pay, including the value of most taxable fringe benefits (for example, a company car). If you're self-employed, net relevant earnings basically means your profits for tax purposes. The limits tell you the maximum *before-tax-relief* amount that you can pay into your personal plan. Table 6.3 shows the contribution limits for new-style personal plans.

Table 6.3: Tax-relief limits on contributions to new-style pension plans [1]

Your age at the start of the tax year (6 April)	Contribution limit as a percentage of your earnings	Contribution limit on £££ for each £1,000 of your earnings
Up to 35	17.5%	£175
36 to 45	20%	£200
46 to 50	25%	£250
51 to 55	30%	£300
56 to 60	35%	£350
61 to 74	40%	£400
75 and over	you can no longer contribute	

[1] Personal pension plans taken out on or after 1 July 1988

In addition to the percentages listed above, there is an overall cash limit on the amount of earnings which can be taken into account in working out your contribution limit. In the 1994–95 tax year, the proposed earnings limit is £76,800. This means, for example, that someone aged 35 earning £80,000 can contribute at most 17.5 per cent of £76,800, which comes to £13,440. The earnings limit is usually increased each year in line with changes in the Retail Prices Index. Table 6.4 shows the earnings limits which applied in earlier years.

Table 6.4: Earnings limits and impact on contributions

Tax year	Earnings limit £	Maximum contribution for person aged up to 35 £
1988–89	No limit	17.5% of earnings
1989–90	£60,000	£10,500
1990–91´	£64,800	£11,340
1991–92	£71,400	£12,495
1992–93	£75,000	£13,125
1993–94	£75,000	£13,125
1994–95	£76,800	£13,440

If you're an employee, your employer can contribute to a new-style personal pension plan on your behalf, but the amount he or she pays counts towards your contribution limit. If you're using a personal pension plan to contract out of SERPS (see Chapter 7), amounts used for contracting out don't count towards the contribution limit.

Table 6.5, below, shows the contribution limits which apply to old-style personal plans.

Table 6.5: Tax-relief limits on contributions to old-style personal plans [1]

Age at the start of the tax year (6 April)	Amount of relief as a percentage of your earnings	Amount of relief in £££ for each £1,000 of your earnings
Up to 50	17.5%	£175
51 to 55	20%	£200
56 to 60	22.5%	£225
61 to 74	27.5%	£275
75 and over	you can no longer contribute	

[1] Personal pension plans taken out before 1 July 1988

If you're an employee, your employer can't contribute to an old-style personal plan, and these plans can't be used for contracting out. Unlike new-style plans, there is no cash limit on the amount which you can pay into an old-style personal pension plan. Despite this, unless their earnings are high, anyone over 35 will be able to pay more into a new-style plan than an old-style one because the percentage limits for new-style plans are higher. At the proposed 1994–95 cash limit, you'll be

Table 6.6: Maximising your contributions: old- or new-style plan?

Age at the start of the tax year (6 April)	Earnings above which maximum contributions to an old-style personal plan may exceed those to a new-style plan [1]
36 to 45	£87,771
46 to 50	£109,714
51 to 55	£115,200
56 to 60	£119,467
61 to 74	£111,709

[1] Based on 1994–95 contribution limits

able to contribute more to an old-style plan than a new-style one only if your earnings exceed the limits in Table 6.6.

It's possible for you to be paying into new- and old-style plans at the same time. In this situation, the tax-relief limits for each type of plan apply, but, in addition, your total contributions to all your plans usually must not exceed the new-style plan limit – see Example 6.5 below.

EXAMPLE 6.5

Leonard saves for retirement mainly through an old-style personal pension plan which he took out back in 1956 (when old-style plans were first launched). He also started a new-style plan in July 1988. Leonard is 65 now and wants to contribute as much as possible to his plans to boost his income once he retires. His earnings in the 1994–95 tax year are £43,000. He can contribute up to 27.5 per cent of £43,000 = £11,825 to his old-style plan. He can contribute up to 40 per cent of £43,000 = £17,200 to his new-style plan. But his total contributions to both plans can't exceed the new-style plan limit – i.e. £17,200.

He decides to pay the full £11,825 into his old-style plan, which lets him pay up to £17,200 – £11,825 = £5,375 into his new-style plan.

Going over the contribution limits

In general, if you pay more into a new-style personal pension plan than the tax relief rules allow, your excess contributions will be returned to you as soon as the over-payment is spotted. If you're an employee and both you and your employer contribute to the plan, any over-payment will be repaid to you rather than your employer. Excess contributions to an old-style plan may be left invested but they'll be treated as an ordinary investment and won't qualify for the special tax treatment given to pension plans.

However, there are two situations in which you can make contributions which do come to more than your tax-relief limit for a particular tax year. The first is where you use the **carry**

back rule. This allows you to have a contribution that you pay in one tax year treated as if it has been paid in the previous year. You must have enough unused tax-relief limit for the previous year to cover the amount carried back. If you had no net relevant earnings in the previous year, you can carry back the contribution two years. In either case, you get tax relief at the rates which applied in the earlier tax year.

Carrying back contributions can be particularly useful if you're a higher rate taxpayer or self-employed, because you'll usually get the tax relief that you claim more quickly than you would with a contribution which is not carried back (because the relief arises from a revised tax assessment for the earlier year). At present, you won't lose out by carrying back a contribution, but, if the tax climate alters, take care that you don't carry back to a year when tax rates were lower than in the current year. In a situation where the tax rate for the earlier year was higher than the rate for the current year, it would of course be advantageous to carry back a contribution.

EXAMPLE 6.6

Jean's a 50-year-old self-employed graphic designer. She generally pays £1,000 a year into her old-style personal pension plan. In the 1988–89 tax year, she earned more than usual and decided to put a bit more into her plan. Rather than increasing her contribution for that year, Jean asked for an extra £500 to be treated as if she'd paid it in the previous year. Not only did she get tax relief on the contribution within a couple of months, but she also received relief at the higher 27 per cent basic tax rate which applied during 1987–88 instead of the 25 per cent rate which applied in 1988–89.

The second way to contribute more than the current year's tax-relief limit allows is by using the **carry forward** rules. You can do this if you have any unused tax-relief limit from the last six years. You can carry forward the unused relief, and use it now. You must carry forward from the earliest year first. But note that you get relief at the current tax rates – not the tax rates which applied in the earlier years.

Bear in mind that, while you can only benefit from tax relief on your contributions to a pension plan if you pay income tax, the contributions themselves do not have to be paid out of taxed income. So, if you are carrying foward unused tax relief, you can use, say, a redundancy payment or inherited lump sum to use up that relief and invest in a pension plan.

EXAMPLE 6.7

Jean, aged 50 (see Example 6.6), had another good year in 1993–94. She landed a very lucrative contract for an American firm which more than doubled her normal yearly earnings. She decided to put a large part of the extra money into her pension plan, though this took her over the tax-relief limit for that year. But she was able to use previously unused relief from earlier years. Table 6.7 overleaf shows Jean's earnings and tax-relief limits for 1993–94 and the preceding six years.

Jean puts £6,500 into her pension plan in the 1993–94 tax year. This uses up her whole tax relief limit for that year plus £3,420 of relief from earlier years. This uses up all the relief from 1987–88 up to 1991–92, but still leaves £265 unused relief from 1992–93. She can continue to carry this £265 relief forward.

Table 6.7: Jean's earnings and tax-relief limits

Tax year	Jean's earnings	Pension tax-relief limit	Jean's contribu-tions	Unused relief for the year	Relief remaining after 1993–94 contribution
1993–94	£17,600	£3,080	£6,500	£ 0	£ 0
1992–93	£11,800	£2,065	£1,000	£1,065	£265
1991–92	£ 9,600	£1,680	£1,000	£ 680	£ 0
1990–91	£ 9,000	£1,575	£1,000	£ 575	£ 0
1989–90	£ 9,200	£1,610	£1,000	£ 610	£ 0
1988–89	£10,000	£1,750	£1,000	£ 750	£ 0
1987–88	£ 8,600	£1,505	£1,500	£ 5	£ 0

Total unused relief for previous six years: £3,685

Special rules for doctors and dentists

If you're a GP or dentist working in a practice, you count as self-employed for tax purposes. But, unusually, you're eligible to contribute to what is, in effect, an employer pension scheme – the National Health Service (NHS) Superannuation Scheme. *At the same time,* you can contribute to your own personal pension plan, and there are special rules to work out how much you can contribute. As a GP or dentist, you have a choice:

- you can pay into the NHS scheme but give up all tax relief on these contributions. In this case, all your earnings count as net relevant earnings (see p.88); the tax-relief limit for personal plan contributions is then worked out in the normal way. This option can be attractive, because you can effectively base *two* pensions on the same earnings
- you can pay into the NHS scheme and receive tax relief as normal on these contributions. Multiplying the NHS scheme contribution by 16⅔ gives a figure for the earnings which are covered by that scheme. Subtracting this amount from your total earnings leaves the amount of net relevant earnings which can be used as the basis of working out contributions to a personal plan.

If you're a dentist or a GP, you may decide not to join the NHS scheme – or to leave it if you already belong. In that case, you could use all your earnings as a basis for contributions to a personal plan in the normal way. But the NHS scheme is a good one and you're likely to do better by joining it.

If you belong to the NHS scheme, you can make additional voluntary contributions – (AVCs) – see p.76 – as long as your total contributions don't exceed the normal limit applying to an employer scheme, which is usually 15 per cent of your earnings. Your AVCs can be made either to the NHS AVC scheme or to a free-standing AVC scheme. If you do make AVCs, the rules for working out your possible contributions to a personal plan are more complicated than those outlined above.

EXAMPLE 6.8

Derek is a 31-year-old doctor earning £30,000 a year from a thriving group practice. In the 1994–95 tax year, he pays tax at the basic rate of 25 per cent. He pays £1,000 a year into the NHS scheme; this has a six per cent contribution rate, so multiplying by 16⅔ gives an estimate for the amount of Derek's earnings which are covered by the NHS scheme. This figure is £16,666. Derek would like to take out a personal pension plan as well. He has two options:

- he can receive tax relief of £250 (25 per cent of £1,000) on the contribution to the NHS scheme. This means that he'll have net relevant earnings of £30,000 – £16,666 = £13,334 which can be used as a basis of his contributions to a personal plan. His maximum contribution would be £2,333, which would qualify for £583 tax relief. In total, he'd be contributing £3,333 to his pension savings with total tax relief of £833
- alternatively, Derek could give up the £250 tax relief on the NHS scheme contribution. In this case, his full £30,000 earnings would be eligible as a basis for contributions to a personal plan. His maximum contribution would be £5,250 which would qualify for tax relief of £1,313.

If Derek wants to make relatively large savings for retirement, the second option looks promising. But he should consider whether he'd do better by making AVCs to the NHS scheme or a free-standing AVC scheme, instead of taking out a personal plan.

Pension mortgages

It is possible to take out a mortgage to buy your home on the understanding that the amount borrowed will eventually be repaid out of the tax-free lump sum from a pension plan. In essence, this type of mortgage is similar to the familiar 'endowment mortgage' – you pay only the interest on the loan during its lifetime, but also make regular payments into an insurance policy (with an endowment mortgage) or pension plan (in the case of pension mortgage); then, the maturing endowment insurance or, in the case of a pension mortgage, the maturing pension plan, provides the lump sum to pay off the loan. The advantage of a pension mortgage over an endowment one is that your contributions to the pension plan qualify for tax relief, whereas the premiums for endowment insurance do not. Similarly, premiums for life insurance to pay off the mortgage in the event of your death will qualify for tax relief if taken out through a personal pension plan (see p.138).

On the minus side, you must bear in mind that using a pension plan for mortgage purposes must inevitably leave you with less money to finance your retirement. You need to be absolutely sure that you can afford to see your potential retirement funding diverted in this way.

You also need to be certain that you'll be able to make consistently the required payments to the personal pension plan – if you have a very variable income from year to year, a pension mortgage is unlikely to be suitable (and may in any case not be available to you, as the lender will require assurance on your ability to keep up the mortgage). You'll also need to consider what you would do if, at some stage, you wanted to join an employer scheme and were, thus, no longer eligible for a personal pension plan. Could you refinance the mortgage? Would you lose out badly on the pension plan because of surrender penalties (see p.180)?

More information

Plan providers and pension advisers can give you details about particular pension plans, and may be able to help you make your pension choices – see Chapters 13 and 14. See Chapter 15 for what to do if you have a problem concerning a personal pension plan, which the plan provider or your adviser can't resolve. For general information about personal plans, contact the Pensions Information Manager at the Association of British Insurers★.

CHAPTER 7

CONTRACTING OUT OF SERPS

IF YOU'RE an employee earning more than a lower earnings limit (£57 a week in the 1994–95 tax year), you're eligible for the State Earnings Related Pension Scheme (SERPS). As a member of SERPS, at retirement you'll receive a pension which is worked out according to a formula, and depends largely on the average of your earnings during your working life. Chapter 4 describes the scheme in detail. You can opt out of SERPS. This is called **contracting out,** which means that you give up some or all of the state earnings related pension and receive a pension from an employer scheme or a personal plan instead.

How to contract out

Generally, you can choose whether or not to contract out. But if you're an employee belonging to a **contracted-out final pay employer scheme**, the choice has been made for you – the only way to rejoin SERPS would be by leaving your employer scheme. That would not be worth doing just for the sake of contracting back into SERPS. With a **contracted-out money purchase employer scheme**, you may be automatically contracted out, but some employers let individual employees choose whether or not to be contracted out.

If you belong to an employer scheme which isn't contracted out, there are several ways in which you can contract out – and you don't have to leave your employer scheme to do so. If you're not in an employer scheme at all, you can contract out using a personal pension plan. Chart 7.1 summarises your options.

Chart 7.1: How to contract out of SERPS

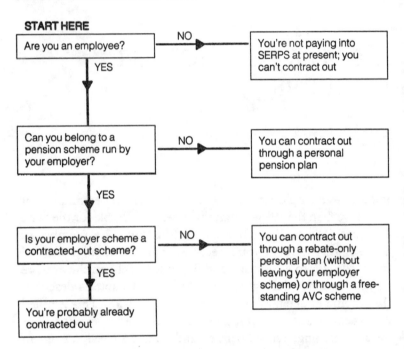

How does contracting out work

Employer final pay schemes

If you're contracted out through your employer's final pay pension scheme (see p.63), both you and your employer pay lower National Insurance on your earnings above the lower earnings limit. This reflects the fact that neither of you is contributing to SERPS during the period for which you're contracted out.

With a final pay scheme, contracting out means that the scheme guarantees to pay you a minimum amount of pension at retirement – **a guaranteed minimum pension (GMP).** It will also pay a guaranteed widow's or widower's pension. Your GMP will be broadly equal to the SERPS pension you'd otherwise have built up. But the precise amount of the GMP doesn't really matter because *you can't lose by contracting out* *through a final pay scheme.* This becomes clear once you look at what happens when you retire.

At retirement, the Department of Social Security (DSS) – the government department responsible for pensions – works out the full SERPS pension you would have got if you hadn't been contracted out at all. From this, it subtracts the amount of any GMPs you qualify for because of periods of contracting out. Whatever remains is the amount of SERPS pension which the state will pay you. If your GMPs are large, you'll receive only a small SERPS pension; if your GMPs are small, you'll receive a larger SERPS pension. But the GMPs plus the SERPS pension you're paid will together always equal the maximum SERPS pension you could have got without contracting out. And if your GMPs come to more than the full SERPS pension, you'll get no SERPS pension, but you'll be better off than you would have been under SERPS. A further aspect of contracting out in this way is that the DSS increases the whole pension (SERPS and GMPs) in line with inflation each year, apart from a small amount of index-linking paid by the employer scheme(s) on GMPs built up since 1988.

You can't lose by contracting out this way and, in practice, you're likely to gain because most employer schemes aim to provide a pension which is greater than just the GMP. You may or may not be required to contribute to the scheme to pay towards the GMP and any extra pension or other benefits.

EXAMPLE 7.1

Alfred (see p.58) retired in May 1994 with a SERPS pension of £45.33 a week – £2,357 a year. Henry is Alfred's twin brother, and in one of those extraordinary coincidences that seem to afflict twins, his yearly earnings were very similar to Alfred's during the last ten years before retirement. However, unlike Alfred, Henry was contracted into SERPS only for the last two years that he worked. For seven years before that, he belonged to a contracted-out final pay scheme (and, before that, he and Alfred ran a small business together). The final pay scheme now pays Henry a GMP of £2,150 a year. This is subtracted from the SERPS pension of £2,357 a year which he would have had if he'd never been contracted out. The remaining £207 (£2,357 less £2,150) is the amount of SERPS pension which he received at retirement. The GMP is increased each year, reflecting part of the effect of inflation. The SERPS pension he gets is increased each year to reflect the full effect of inflation on the SERPS pension and the remaining effect of inflation on his GMP – see p.103.

Employer money purchase schemes

Contracting out through an employer money purchase scheme (see p.64) sometimes called a **COMP** – works quite differently. You and your employer still both pay lower National Insurance on your earnings above the lower earnings limit. But the employer scheme doesn't make any guarantees about the amount of pension it will pay you to replace the SERPS you'd otherwise have been building up. Instead, your employer is required to guarantee that he or she will pay a set amount into the scheme which will be left to build up a fund. The amount invested is equal to the amounts that you and your employer have saved by paying lower National Insurance – it is called the **rebate**. The fund which builds up must be used to provide you with a retirement pension (and a widow's or widower's pension). Your rights to these benefits are called your **protected rights**. How much the protected rights pension will be depends on how well the invested money grows and on the rate – the **annuity rate** – at which the fund can be converted to pension when the time comes for it to be paid.

At retirement, the DSS again works out the full SERPS pension you would have built up if you'd not been contracted out at all. But it then subtracts the amount of the GMP you would have built up if, during the period you were contracted out, you'd belonged to a contracted-out final pay scheme. This is called a **notional GMP** and it may be more or less than the actual pension that you receive from the contracted-out money purchase scheme.

If your invested fund grows well and annuity rates are favourable when you come to retire, contracting out through an employer money purchase scheme may mean that you end up with more pension than you would have done had you stayed in SERPS. But, if your invested fund does badly and annuity rates are low when you retire, you may find with hindsight that you'd have been better off staying in SERPS. You take a gamble (though the gamble will be small in some cases – see p.106).

A COMP scheme can be designed to accept contributions paid by your employer, as well as just the rebate, and your employer may or may not require you to make contributions.

In practice, COMP schemes have proved complicated to run and some employers have found it easier to help those employees who want to contract out to do so via a personal pension plan. (Personal pension plans can also be set up on a 'group basis', with the employer arranging common terms for the plans and perhaps making contributions to them.) From 1993–94 onwards, personal pension plans have a financial advantage over contracted-out money purchase plans (see p.106). All these factors suggest that COMP schemes will become increasingly rare.

EXAMPLE 7.2

Jacky is 25. She has just started work as a receptionist with a firm of office equipment suppliers on a salary of £12,000 a year. The firm has recently set up a contracted-out money purchase (COMP) scheme which Jacky has decided to join. Until now, she's made no savings for retirement apart from contributions to the state basic and SERPS pensions through paying National Insurance.

To work out whether Jacky's decision is a good one, various assumptions need to be made about her future earnings, future investment returns and future annuity rates. Suppose that by contracting out in the 1994–95 tax year, Jacky gives up £37 a year (in today's money) of her eventual SERPS pension. On modest assumptions, that year's contributions to the COMP scheme might provide a pension at retirement of, say, £50 a year (in today's money). Since this is greater than the SERPS pension given up, contracting out through the COMP scheme looks to be a good idea for Jacky in 1994–95.

Personal pension plans

If you contract out through a personal pension plan – called an **appropriate personal pension** – you and your employer carry on paying National Insurance at the full rate on all your earnings, but the DSS repays part of it – called the **rebate** – which is paid directly into your personal pension plan. The rebate is invested to build up a fund which will be used to provide you with a retirement pension (and a widow's or widower's pension) in place of the SERPS pension you'd otherwise have built up. Your rights to these benefits are called your **protected rights**. The amount of protected rights pension your plan provides depends on how well the invested rebate grows and annuity rates at the time you retire.

As with contracting out through an employer money purchase scheme, at retirement the DSS works out the full SERPS pension that you could have built up and then subtracts notional GMPs corresponding to periods when you were contracted out. Depending on how well your personal plan has performed, the notional GMPs may be greater or smaller than the actual pension your plan provides. Once again, contracting out means that you could end up with more or with less pension than if you'd stayed in SERPS.

An appropriate personal pension is technically a single lump sum contribution plan which may accept only the amount of the rebate, any incentive (see p.106) and any related tax relief (see p.108). If you belong to an employer pension scheme, and simultaneously contract out using a personal plan, you can only have an appropriate pension plan – called a **rebate-only plan** or **minimum appropriate personal pension**. But, if you don't belong to an employer scheme, your appropriate plan can form part of a personal pension plan package which receives contributions greater than just the rebate.

Free-standing AVC schemes

If you belong to an employer scheme which is not contracted out you can contract out independently using a free-standing additional voluntary contribution (FSAVC) scheme (see p.76), instead of a personal pension plan. But, in practice, you'll usually do better to choose the personal pension plan route, because a quirk in the tax rules (see p.109) means that the DSS pays less into a contracted-out free-standing AVC scheme than it pays into a contracted-out personal plan.

Pension increases

After retirement, SERPS pensions are increased each year in line with changes in the Retail Prices Index. If you're contracted out, the state used to continue to provide the full increase required to keep your SERPS and GMPs growing in line with inflation. But this has now changed: the scheme providing a contracted-out pension, or the plan provider, must increase the pension at a rate of three per cent a year, or by the rate of inflation if this is less. This change affects employer pensions for people retiring on or after 6 April 1990, but only for GMPs built up since 6 April 1988. It affects personal pensions built up from 1 July 1988 onwards.

Each year, the DSS recalculates the amount of SERPS it must pay you by subtracting your GMPs or notional GMPs from the full SERPS pension that you could theoretically have built up. But the figures used in the calculation will have been revised to take account of the inflation-proofing. The full SERPS pension will have been increased in line with the change in the Retail Prices Index. The GMPs and notional GMPs built up since 1988 will have been increased each time by three per cent a year. The result of these yearly revisions is that, if contracting out left you at the start of retirement with a lower pension than you'd otherwise have got, the shortfall will increase year by year. But, if contracting out left you better off, the excess will increase each year.

Should you contract out?

SERPS provides a pension which is linked to your earnings and keeps pace with changes in national earnings up to retirement and with changes in prices after retirement. If you're contracted out through an employer final pay scheme, you lose none of this and it makes little odds whether you're in SERPS or out. But, if the final pay route isn't open to you, should you contract out? Is it worth giving up the security of SERPS for the opportunities, but uncertainties, of contracting out? The answer depends largely on four factors:

- your sex
- your age
- your view about future investment performance
- the size of the rebate and any incentive payment.

Your sex

Men and women, on average, don't benefit equally from SERPS. Any woman born before 6 April 1955 will have a lower state pension age than for a man. Also, women in their mid-sixties can expect to live some three or four years longer than a man of the same age. So, supposing a man and a woman had identical entitlements to SERPS at the start of their retirements, the woman could expect to receive her pension for between three and eight years longer than the man. If the woman were currently in her late forties or older, she could expect to receive considerably more SERPS than the man. A younger woman would not do quite as well, but would still tend to do better than the man. Despite this difference in the total amount of pension a man and a woman can expect to receive, the rebate to be invested in a COMP scheme or a personal plan is identical for a man and a woman who earn the same. Yet, other factors being equal, the woman is giving up more SERPS than the man. The upshot of this is that contracting out is more likely to be attractive to men than to women.

Your age

SERPS pension is worked out according to a formula, but a contracted-out money purchase pension – such as that provided by a COMP scheme or a personal plan – depends to a large extent on how the invested rebates grow. If you're young, you have a long time until you reach pension age: your rebates will be invested for a longer period, and should grow by more than the rebates of an older person who'll reach retirement sooner.

In addition, SERPS pensions are being cut back for people retiring after the end of this century. The cut-backs are being phased in gradually, with the result that the earlier you reach state pension age (in other words, the older you are), the more SERPS pension you would give up through contracting out, compared with a younger person. Since you receive the same rate of rebate regardless of age, contracting out is more attractive the younger you are.

Your view about future investment performance

With contracted-out money purchase pensions, investment performance will play a large part in determining how large or small your eventual pension will be. If you're optimistic on this score, and expect your invested rebates to grow well, contracting out will tend to be an attractive option. If, on the other hand, you take a more cautious view of likely investment growth, you'll be more attracted to staying in SERPS.

The size of the rebate

The size of the rebate is set by the government on the advice of its actuary. (An actuary is a professional whose skills lie in assessing probabilities and likely future values from statistical and other data.) The amount of the rebate is supposed roughly to represent the cost of buying a GMP for an average member of a large employer final pay scheme.

The rebate was set for the five years from April 1988 to April 1993 at a total of 5.8 per cent of earnings above the lower earnings limit (see p.32) up to the upper earnings limit (see p.52) – sometimes referred to as 5.8 per cent of **upper band earnings**. Of this, 2 per cent represented a rebate of the National Insurance you paid; 3.8 per cent represented a rebate of the National Insurance paid on your behalf by your employer. If you had not already been contracted out of SERPS, then in the five years up to 5 April 1993, you also qualified for a special incentive bonus which equalled a further 2 per cent of your middle band earnings.

Revised rebates apply from 6 April 1993 for three years – i.e. until 5 April 1996, when they will be revised again. From 6 April 1993, the overall rebate has been set at a reduced rate of 4.8 per cent of upper band earnings. Of this, 1.8 per cent represents a rebate of your National Insurance and 3 per cent that of your employer. In addition, there is a 1 per cent incentive payable to everyone aged 30 or over who is contracted out through a personal pension plan.

It is worth stressing that the incentive payment is no longer linked to being *newly* contracted out and it is not available to people who are contracted out in ways other than through a personal pension plan. This gives personal plans a clear advantage over contracting out through an employer scheme and is likely to encourage a further decline in the use of COMP schemes (see p.100).

Table 7.1 on p.110 gives a guide to the amount of £££ of rebate that would be paid into a COMP scheme run by your employer, or your contracted-out personal plan, depending on how much you earn. Obviously, the more that is invested in your contracted-out scheme or plan, the larger the amount of the eventual fund available to provide your pension. If you qualify for the incentive payment, contracting out will be more attractive than if you don't.

The factors combined

Combining the four factors tells you that if you are male, young, and optimistic about future investment growth, con-tracting out is likely to be a good move. If you're female, no longer so young and a pessimist, you'd be better off staying in SERPS. Given the current rebates, if you do not qualify for the one per cent incentive, you're probably better off contracted out of SERPS up to the age of 30 or so, but, after that, you should consider staying in or rejoining SERPS. If you do qualify for the incentive, then contracting out may make sense up to your late thirties if you're a woman, and maybe 40 if you're a man; after that, consider contracting back in or staying in. These 'pivotal' ages can't be clear cut – they are heavily dependent on the various assumptions made. If you are doubtful about what action to take, consider getting professional advice – see p.111.

The pivotal ages are valid only while the rebate is at its present level. After 5 April 1996, the level of rebate will change. Moreover, it looks as if the government may switch to a system of age-related rebates with smaller rebates being paid to younger people and larger amounts to older people. Other factors may also change – for example, your view about investment growth. So you should periodically review your contracting-out decision.

At present, you can contract out now, but contract back into SERPS at a later date. So there's nothing to stop you taking advantage of a contracted-out scheme or plan now, but rejoining SERPS when, for example, you get to an age at which SERPS benefits look more advantageous.

A note of caution

According to the *National Association of Pension Funds survey* (see p.72), over 80 per cent of the employer schemes surveyed are contracted out of SERPS. If you belong to a large final pay scheme, you're particularly likely to be contracted out through the scheme. Bear in mind that you can't lose by contracting out on a final pay basis – there's no need for you to consider contracting back in.

If you're contracted out through a COMP scheme but find yourself in the group which would probably be better off contracted into SERPS, you should think carefully before making any decision. You may be able to contract in without leaving the scheme, depending on the scheme rules. If you can't do that, you'll be able to contract in only by leaving the employer scheme. But the scheme may be providing more generous benefits than just those required by the contracting-out rules. Leaving the scheme might mean you give up more than you gain by contracting back into SERPS. If in doubt, talk to the scheme officials (see p.80) and consider getting independent advice (see p.111).

Tax relief on your rebate

Employer pension schemes

Contracting out through an employer pension scheme doesn't normally affect your income tax position: you pay less in National Insurance, but the earnings used as a basis for working out income tax are unchanged. If, however, your employer requires you to contribute to the pension scheme part of what you have saved by having to pay less National Insurance, the amount you contribute will be treated as a normal pension contribution for tax purposes. This means that the amount will be deducted from your pay before income tax is worked out, so you automatically get tax relief on the contribution at your highest rate (or rates) of tax.

Personal pension plans

Special tax rules apply to the rebate paid into a personal pension plan. You are given tax relief on the part of the rebate which represents your own National Insurance (in other words, 1.8 per cent of earnings between the upper and lower earnings limits given the present level of rebate). Tax relief is given only at the basic rate – even if you're a higher rate taxpayer. You don't receive the tax relief directly; instead, it's paid by the DSS into your personal pension plan along with the rebate. The tax relief represents another 0.6 per cent of your earnings between the upper and lower earnings limits. There's no tax relief on any incentive payment, and there's no relief on the part of the rebate which represents National Insurance paid by your employer.

EXAMPLE 7.3

Ryan, who is 45 and a higher-rate taxpayer earning considerably more than the upper earnings limit for National Insurance, saves for retirement through a personal pension plan (see p.88) and also has a separate appropriate personal pension to contract him out of SERPS. Ryan pays nothing directly to the appropriate plan but, after the end of each tax year, the Department of Social Security (DSS) pays an amount into it. For the 1994–95 tax year, the DSS pays in £1,241. This is made up of the following sums:

Rebate of Ryan's National Insurance	£ 349
Rebate of his employer's National Insurance	£ 582
1% incentive payment	£ 194
Basic rate tax relief on rebate of Ryan's National Insurance	£ 116
TOTAL	£1,241

Free-standing AVC schemes

There's no tax relief on any part of the rebate paid into a free-standing AVC scheme, whereas you do get some tax relief when you contract out through a personal pension plan (see above). Since, in other respects, a contracted-out free-standing AVC scheme is virtually identical to a contracted-out personal pension plan, there's usually no advantage in choosing the free-standing AVC route. However, if you're already contributing to a free-standing AVC scheme, contracting out through it may be convenient for you, and you might save in plan charges (see p.178) compared with contracting out through a separate personal pension plan.

How much is paid into your scheme or plan?

If you're contracted out through an employer final pay scheme, your employer must make sure that enough is paid into the scheme eventually to provide at least the guaranteed amount of pension. Usually, any contribution you pay will be a set proportion (or set amount) of your salary. The employer will vary his or her contribution as necessary to ensure that the total being paid into the scheme is sufficient.

Table 7.1: What the government pays towards your COMP pension or personal pension for the 1994–95 tax year [1]

Yearly earnings	Payment to an employer COMP scheme [2]	Payment to a contracted personal pension plan [3]	
		No incentive	*With 1% incentive*
£	£	£	£
Under £2,964 [4]	0	0	0
£ 5,000	98	110	130
£10,000	338	380	450
£11,000	386	434	514
£12,000	434	488	578
£13,000	482	542	642
£14,000	530	596	706
£15,000	578	650	770
£16,000	626	704	834
£17,000	674	758	898
£18,000	722	812	962
£19,000	770	866	1,026
£20,000	818	920	1,090
£21,000	866	974	1,154
£22,360 and over [5]	931	1,047	1,241

[1] Rounded to the nearest £. Note that rebates are actually paid during the following tax year
[2] Based on a rebate of 4.8% of earnings between the lower and upper earnings limits. Tax relief, if any, is paid to you, not into the scheme
[3] Based on a rebate of 4.8% of earnings between the lower and upper earnings limits plus tax relief on part of the rebate equal to 0.6% of earnings between the two levels. (Based on basic rate tax of 25% in 1994–95.) The rebate becomes 5.8% plus 0.6% tax when the 1% incentive is available
[4] This is the lower earnings limit for the 1994–95 tax year
[5] This is the upper earnings limit for the 1994–95 tax year

The position with an employer COMP scheme, or a personal pension plan, is rather different. The amount of the eventual pension is not guaranteed; instead, a minimum amount must be invested. The minimum must equal the rebate plus any incentive plus, in the case of personal plans, the tax relief provided by the government. Table 7.1 above shows these minimum amounts for the 1994–95 tax year, depending on the level of your earnings.

More information

You may feel that the decision about whether to be contracted in or contracted out of SERPS is reasonably clear for you, or you may be contracted out on a final pay basis in which case you do not need to take any action. But, if you're in that grey area where it's not clear whether contracting out is worthwhile for you, you'll need some help in making your decision.

A personal pension plan provider will give you an illustration of the possible pension from an appropriate personal pension (based on standard assumptions which he or she is legally obliged to use). Most providers will include with the illustration an estimate of the SERPS pension you would be giving up by contracting out. Bear in mind that illustrations give you *informed guesses* – it's impossible to know what the future benefits from a plan or from SERPS will be. See Chapter 14 for more details about personal plan illustrations.

If you belong to, or could join, an employer pension scheme, you could ask the pension scheme administrators or trustees (see p.80) to advise you – and they may be able to call on the services of a pensions consultant.

In an ideal world, it would also be sensible to get some completely independent advice. Independent advice about contracting out, and about any other aspect of your pension choices, is available from actuaries and from expert pensions consultants, but it's usually fairly expensive. Normally, you'll pay a fee based on the time spent on your case. You should establish the likely cost of the advice before going ahead. If independent advice is too costly for you alone, could you perhaps join forces with colleagues in a similar position and spread the cost between you? You can obtain a list of members of the following professional bodies, who provide independent advice, from the Society of Pension Consultants★ and the Association of Consulting Actuaries★.

CHAPTER 8

LEAVING A PENSION ARRANGEMENT BEFORE RETIREMENT

A GREAT advantage of a personal pension plan is that it is personal to *you* and can be quite independent of *your job*. But employer schemes are inevitably linked to your work, and changing jobs will affect your pension planning. Your employer pension will be similarly affected if you decide to opt out of the employer scheme, even though you're not leaving the job.

If you have a personal plan, beware of switching to another, or of stopping a regular payment plan – there may be heavy penalties which severely reduce the amount of your savings, and with each new plan, you'll incur fresh charges.

Your right to a pension from an employer scheme

If you leave an employer pension scheme and you've been a member of it for two years or more, the scheme *must* either provide you with a pension at retirement – called a **preserved** or **deferred pension** – or allow you to transfer your pension rights to another pension scheme or plan.

Taking a refund

If you leave a scheme that you've belonged to for less than two years, you're not automatically entitled to any pension rights at all. More likely, you'll get a refund of your contributions if it was a contributory scheme. You can have back only contributions which you paid *yourself* – not any contributions paid on your behalf by your employer. The trustees of the scheme have to hand over to the Inland Revenue tax on your refund, and usually the amount of the tax will be deducted from what you get. From the 1988–89 tax year onwards, the tax is paid at a special rate of 20 per cent (10 per cent in earlier years). If you're a non-taxpayer, you can't reclaim the tax; on the other hand, if you *are* a taxpayer, there's no more tax to pay.

There may also be a deduction – usually quite large – if you had been contracted out of SERPS through the employer scheme. The scheme may arrange to 'buy you back' into the state scheme for the period you had been contracted out. The scheme has to pay over a sum of money – called the **contributions equivalent premium** – to the state, and part of this amount will be subtracted from your refund. The deduction is made before tax on the refund is worked out.

Your refund might include interest on your contributions – though often at a very modest rate. If your scheme usually adds interest and at a reasonable rate, this can make the scheme a good place even for short-term investment: if you're at least a basic rate taxpayer, you'll have had tax relief at your full rate on the money you invested (your contributions) and your return is taxed at only 20 per cent – less than your normal rate.

If you've had a refund relating to a period that you'd been in an employer scheme, the Inland Revenue deems that your earnings for that period are no longer covered by any pension arrangement. You can, instead, take out a personal pension plan to cover the period using the **carry forward rules** (see p.92), as long as you do so within the time limits those rules allow. The tax rules let you have a refund of contributions that you made before 6 April 1975 regardless of how long you've been a member of your employer pension scheme, but this is unlikely to be a wise move in view of the pension rights you'd lose.

Leaving an employer final pay pension scheme

If you've been in an employer final pay scheme (see p.63) for two years or more, on leaving, the scheme must provide you with a preserved pension, or let you transfer your pension rights to another pension scheme or plan.

In a final pay scheme, your pension is worked out according to a formula, and is based on your years in the scheme (or working for the employer) and your pay. If you stay in the scheme until retirement, your pay at that time is used in the calculation. But, if you leave before retirement, it's usually your pay at the time you leave that is relevant. Even ignoring inflation, in many cases, your pay as an 'early leaver' will be less than your pay at retirement would have been, because you'd normally expect pay increases due, for example, to promotion. This is one reason why changing jobs can result in you losing pension.

EXAMPLE 8.1

Harriet, who works for a firm of accountants, has been a member of its pension scheme for four years. This is a final pay scheme which bases pensions on one-sixtieth of final pay for each year in the scheme. Harriet earns £16,200 a year at present. With promotion, she would hope to earn at least £60,000 a year, in terms of today's money, by the time she reaches retirement. If her final pay at retirement did turn out to be £60,000 a year, her four years to date in the scheme would be worth a pension of 4 × $\frac{1}{60}$ × £60,000 = £4,000 a year in today's money. But Harriet is thinking about leaving accountancy and taking a job that follows her interest in art instead. If she leaves the firm's pension scheme now, her four years will have earned her a preserved pension of only 4 × $\frac{1}{60}$ × £16,200 = £1,080 a year. The preserved pension must be increased to protect it at least partially against inflation (see below). Whether Harriet gains or loses pension because of her job move depends on many factors, including inflation, her prospects in her new job, her new pension arrangements, and so on.

The effect of inflation

There is a second way in which you may lose pension if you leave a final pay scheme before retirement. If you've left an employer pension scheme before 1 January 1986, the scheme is under no obligation at all to increase your preserved pension (other than contracted-out pension rights – see below) between the time you left and the time when it will eventually be paid to you. Inflation severely eats into the buying power of these unprotected preserved pensions.

For people leaving an employer scheme on or after 1 January 1991, pension rights they have built up must be at least partly protected against inflation. This is done by requiring the scheme to increase the preserved pension in line with inflation up to five per cent a year (but see below for the rules concerning contracted-out pension rights). Your preserved pension is still at the mercy of inflation if prices rise on average by more than five per cent a year, and, historically, earnings have tended to rise faster than prices, so the link to price inflation may still mean that your pension lags behind. In its 1992 annual survey, the National Association of Pension Funds found that just over a sixth of schemes surveyed increased preserved pensions by more than the amount required by law.

Contracted-out pension rights

If you're contracted out through a final pay scheme which you then leave, the scheme is obliged to protect your contracted-out pension rights – in other words, your guaranteed minimum pension (GMP) and widow's or widower's GMP. The amount of GMP you're entitled to at the time you leave is calculated. It must then be increased until the time at which you reach the state pension age. The scheme can choose one of three ways in which to make the increases:

- in line with increases in national average earnings
- by a fixed amount of 7.5 per cent a year (8.5 per cent for people who left a scheme before 6 April 1988)
- in line with earnings inflation up to a maximum of five per cent, as long as the scheme makes a payment to the State called a **limited revaluation premium**.

If, with the last two methods, the revalued GMPs fall short of GMPs increased in line with average earnings in the nation as a whole, the state makes good the shortfall through SERPS.

GMPs can be transferred to another pension scheme or plan, as long as that scheme or plan can be used for contracted-out pension rights (see p. 121).

Leaving an employer money purchase scheme

If you leave an employer money purchase scheme after two years' membership or more, you stop contributing to the scheme, and your employer stops making contributions on your behalf. But the money already invested continues to grow as before, and you'll get the full benefit of the fund which has built up by the time you come to retire. Alternatively, you can transfer the fund which has built up to another pension scheme or plan.

The amount in a money purchase preserved fund is quite independent of your level of pay on leaving, and doesn't suffer from the potential drawbacks of a final pay preserved pension (see p. 113), in that you shouldn't generally lose pension if you're an early leaver from a money purchase scheme, compared with the amount you would have had in respect of those years if you'd stayed. However, it should be borne in mind that even an 'early leaver's' pension rights from a money purchase scheme could be less than the entitlement that might have been built up over the same period in a final pay scheme.

Staying in touch with an employer scheme

If you decide to leave your preserved pension with the pension scheme of an employer you've left, be sure to let the scheme know whenever you change address. You should also keep track of the benefits you can expect from the scheme at retirement (or if you decide to take a transfer at some stage). The scheme administrators are not obliged to send you benefit statements (see p. 79) automatically, but you have the right to request a statement as often as once every 12 months. Once requested, the scheme administrators should provide a statement within two months.

Changing jobs if you have a personal plan

If you have a single lump sum contribution personal pension plan, changing jobs has no effect at all on the plan. And, if you have a regular contribution personal plan, you can usually keep your plan going without any alteration if you change jobs. There are three exceptions:

- if you have a contracted-out personal plan (see Chapter 7) for which you cease to be eligible. This would happen if you switched from being an employee to self-employed status instead. It would also happen if you decided to join a new employer scheme which was itself a contracted-out scheme. In both cases, you would not be able to continue claiming the National Insurance rebate for your personal plan
- if you have a (non-contracted-out) personal plan for which you cease to be eligible. This would happen if your new employer runs a pension scheme which you decide to join. You can't simultaneously belong to an employer scheme and have a personal plan (except in the circumstances outlined on p.81)
- if your old employer has been paying some or all of the contributions to your personal plan. You'll need to investigate whether you can keep the plan going with lower contributions, with contributions from your new employer, or by paying in more yourself.

If you do have to stop paying into your personal plan, you can't get back any money already paid into it, except as a pension (and any tax-free lump sum for which you're eligible) at your pension age. To do this, you must have reached at least the earliest pension age recognised by the tax rules and the plan provider.

If you stop paying into a regular payment personal plan, usually your fund continues to be invested, and it carries on growing as before to provide your eventual pension and any other benefits. Alternatively, you can transfer the fund to another pension plan or scheme – for example, you might want to invest it in your new employer scheme (assuming the scheme will accept your transfer). Likewise, you can transfer the fund built up in a single contribution personal plan, if you wish.

If you have to stop paying into a regular contribution plan, the eventual pension will of course be smaller than originally expected, because you'll have put less money into the plan. However, if you stop paying in the early years, the most severe effect will be due to charges. There are a variety of charges (see p.178). These give the plan provider its profit margin, and cover its costs which are usually particularly heavy when the plan is first set up (see p.193). If you keep up the plan as originally intended, the charges are effectively spread over a long period of time and have a proportionately small impact on your overall return. But, if you stop the plan in the early years, a large chunk of the charges will usually be set against your fund – which is as yet relatively small. This can drastically reduce the amount in your plan and, in some cases, can reduce your fund to nothing. With some plans, charges continue to erode the value of your fund after you've stopped paying in, thus reducing it further. So you'll need to look at the terms of your particular plan very carefully in this situation in order to decide whether you should leave any value remaining invested in the plan or transfer it elsewhere.

Transferring your pension rights

Since 1 January 1986, anyone leaving an employer pension scheme who has a right to a preserved pension also has the right to take a **transfer value** instead. A transfer value is a lump sum which is judged to be equivalent to the preserved pension (and any other rights) given up. You can't receive the transfer value as cash in hand, though – it must be reinvested in another pension scheme or plan.

Both old– and new–style personal pension plans must also give you the right to a transfer value, if you wish to switch the fund you have built up to another pension arrangement.

There are a variety of ways in which you can reinvest a transfer value – they are summarised in Table 8.1 opposite. But note that, while all employer schemes and new–style personal pension plans must give you the right to *take* a transfer value, there is no obligation on any scheme or plan to *accept* your transfer value.

Table 8.1: Transferring your pension savings

Your current method of pension saving	Your transfer choices
Old-style personal plan	New-style personal plan *or* employer scheme
New-style personal plan – not contracted out	Another new-style plan *or* employer scheme
New-style personal plan – contracted out	Another contracted-out new-style personal plan *or* contracted-out employer scheme
Employer scheme – not contracted out	Another employer scheme *or* new-style personal plan *or* section 32 plan (see p.122)
Employer scheme – contracted out	Another contracted-out employer scheme *or* contracted-in employer scheme [1] *or* contracted-out new-style personal plan *or* section 32 plan (see p.122)

[1] In which case your old scheme may still pay your eventual GMP or you may be bought back into SERPS

How much is the transfer value

If you are switching your pension rights from an employer money purchase scheme, or a personal pension plan (which also works on the money purchase basis), the transfer value is simply the value of your fund – in other words, the contributions plus their investment growth less any deductions for charges and expenses.

If you are switching from a final pay scheme, the transfer value must be worked out by the scheme's actuary. He or she makes assumptions, for example, about future investment growth, and works back to arrive at a lump sum which, if invested now, could reasonably be expected to produce enough to pay the amount of your preserved pension at retirement (together with any other rights, such as widow's or widower's pensions, guaranteed pension increases, and so on). The figure for the lump sum is the amount of your transfer value.

As the transfer value is the cash equivalent of your pension

119

rights, a transfer value relating to a final pay scheme incorporates any 'loss' you might be making as a result of leaving the scheme early.

What will the transfer value buy?

If you're transferring into a money purchase pension scheme or plan, the transfer value will simply be added to your fund and invested until it is used to provide your retirement pension or other benefits.

If you're transferring into a final pay scheme, the transfer value might be used in a number of ways, for example:

- it could be used now to 'buy' a fixed amount of pension at retirement
- it could be used now to buy 'extra years' in the scheme, so that you're credited with more years of membership than you will have in reality. Via the pension formula, these years are translated into a higher pension and other benefits
- it could be invested as a separate fund to be used at retirement to 'buy' extra benefits in the main scheme – in a similar way to an AVC scheme.

Buying extra years, in particular, often causes some confusion, because the number of years credited in the new scheme is invariably less than the number of years you had belonged to the old scheme. But it's easy to see why the difference arises: the transfer value from the old scheme reflects your preserved pension. In the case of a final pay scheme, this was based on the pay when you left the scheme and the amount by which the preserved pension will be increased up to retirement. In the new scheme, your transfer value is used to 'buy' an equivalent amount of pension, but, this time, it will be based on your expected pay at retirement. Since this is generally higher than your pay on leaving the old scheme, the transfer value equates to fewer years in the new scheme than in the old. Similarly, if the new scheme offers more generous benefits (for example, better widow's pension, higher increases to pensions after retirement), your transfer value will buy fewer years in the new scheme than the old.

EXAMPLE 8.2

Harriet decides to leave the accountancy firm for which she works. After a year of trying to get a job in the art world, she decides to return to finance and joins a large merchant banking conglomerate. Her new employer runs a final pay pension scheme, which will accept a transfer value from Harriet's old employer scheme. For simplicity, this example ignores the increases which must by law be made to Harriet's preserved pension, so we'll assume that her four years in the old pension scheme are worth a preserved pension of £1,080 a year (in today's money). The actuary of the old scheme calculates that a lump sum of £5,600 would, if invested now, be enough to provide that pension. In the new scheme, it's estimated that her pay at retirement might be £25,000 (in today's money). Thus, each year in the new scheme would provide her with $\frac{1}{60} \times £25,000 = £417$. The actuary of the new scheme works out that the transfer value is just about enough to buy two-and-a-half years' worth of future pension. So Harriet gives up four years of membership in her old scheme for just two-and-a-half years in the new scheme, but the preserved pension of £1,080 a year she gives up is, in this case, virtually identical to the £1,079 a year pension she is expected to get from the new scheme as a result of the two-and-a-half years with which she's credited.

Transferring contracted-out pension rights

The guarantees associated with contracting out must continue even if the benefits are transferred. This is the case whether you're contracted out through a final pay scheme which provides a guaranteed minimum pension (GMP), or through a money purchase arrangement which merely guarantees that minimum contributions will be used to provide the protected rights (see Chapter 7).

If you're contracted out, you can transfer your contracted-out pension rights to a new employer contracted-out scheme, to a section 32 plan (see over), or to an appropriate personal pension plan. If you transfer from a contracted-out final pay scheme to a money purchase scheme or plan, you'll lose the right to a GMP – instead, you'll get money purchase contracted-out rights. In other words, the transfer value of the GMP will have to be invested to provide the protected rights pensions – a retirement pension and a widow's or widower's pension.

If you transfer the rest of your pension rights to a new employer scheme which is contracted in and thus can't accept contracted-out rights, your old scheme can either continue to preserve just your GMP, or it can arrange for you to be 'bought back' into the state scheme by paying a **transfer premium** to the state. If you're 'bought back' in this way, you'll no longer get a GMP at retirement from the old employer scheme; instead, you'll get SERPS pension from the state.

Transferring to a section 32 plan

Section 32 plans – also called **buy-out bonds** – are a special type of personal pension plan designed to accept transfer values from employer pension schemes. The transfer value is paid into the plan and used to buy a deferred annuity (an insurance product designed to pay out an income starting at some future date). The fund which builds up is then used to provide a retirement pension and any other benefits. Section 32 plans were first introduced in 1981; since July 1988, new-style personal pension plans have provided an alternative to them.

Section 32 plans can be used to preserve contracted-out pension rights, and can be a good idea in the case of transfers from contracted-out final pay schemes. The section 32 plan must take over the guarantee to provide a set amount of GMP at retirement. To do this, the plan provider needs to be satisfied that the transfer value is sufficient. By contrast, if you transfer from a contracted-out final pay scheme to a contracted-out new-style personal plan, you give up your right to a guaranteed amount of pension, though you get protected rights instead. With a personal plan, you take the risk that the transfer value might provide a smaller pension than the GMP you gave up; with a section 32 plan, the plan provider takes that risk.

Winding up

If your employer scheme is wound up (for example, in the event of your employer going bust, or being taken over by another firm which doesn't wish to continue the scheme), your pension entitlement from the scheme depends on the scheme's rules. Some schemes are fairly generous to members in the event of winding up, but with others, you may be *entitled* only to the minimum required under the law – i.e. the benefits that an early leaver could get. Rather than making promises about benefits, the scheme rules may give the trustees (see p.152) discretion to decide what benefits over and above the legal minimum are provided, in which case you will be dependent on the health of the pension fund and the priority given to paying or increasing the benefits of different types of members – usually those currently receiving pensions will be given top priority, if funds are short.

Since 1 July 1992, regulations have come into effect which, for final pay schemes (and any schemes with a final **pay** element), make any shortfall in the pension fund a debt of the employer. Where the employer has gone bust, the debt will rank alongside other unsecured creditors who are owed money. This gives scheme members a better chance of getting their rights than in the past, but – if the employer doesn't have the money – they will continue to lose out.

CHAPTER 9

HELP IN THE EVENT OF DEATH

PENSION schemes don't just provide you with an income in old age. They can also be used to provide financial support for your widow, widower, children and other dependants in the event of your death. Sometimes these benefits form an automatic part of the pension scheme or plan; sometimes they are optional extras.

What the state provides for widows

What help your widow could get from the state in the event of your death depends on the record of National Insurance you'd built up. Assuming you'd paid enough contributions – see Chart 9.1 on p.126 – she could be entitled to some or all of the following state benefits:

- **widow's payment** This is a tax-free lump sum of £1,000
- **widowed mother's allowance** This is a regular income that your widow can get if she is caring for your children
- **widow's pension** This is a regular income for widows aged 45 or more who haven't any dependent children.

Chart 9.1 summarises the state help available for widows.

The amount of the widow's payment has not changed since it was introduced in April 1988, but the widowed mother's allowance and widow's pension are both increased each year in line with changes in the Retail Prices Index – in common with other state pensions. There's no tax to pay on the widow's payment, but widowed mother's allowance and widow's pension both count as income for tax purposes.

Help for your widow if you have dependent children

Whether or not you have children, your widow can receive the widow's payment provided she is under 60 and you were not receiving (or eligible for) a basic state retirement pension. She will be eligible for the widowed mother's allowance if you have a dependent child or children. A child is dependent if your widow can claim child benefit (see below) for him or her – this will be the case for most children up to the age of 18. Your widow usually continues to get the allowance for as long as she is caring for the children. But the allowance stops if she remarries. When the youngest child no longer counts as dependent, your widow may be able to get a widow's pension (see below) instead.

In the 1994–95 tax year, the full widowed mother's allowance is £57.60 a week plus £11 a week for each child. On top of this, your widow receives any State Earnings Related Pension Scheme (SERPS) pension that you've built up (see Chapter 4). The SERPS pension is reduced if she can get a contracted-out widow's pension from your employer pension scheme (see p.132) or your personal pension plan (see p.137).

Your widow will normally carry on getting **child benefit** for each of your children under the age of 19. This is £10.20 a week for your only or eldest child and £8.25 a week for each subsequent child in the 1994–95 tax year. If both child benefit and extra widowed mother's allowance are payable in respect of the only or eldest child, the child dependency part of the widowed mother's allowance will be reduced to £9.80 in the 1994–95 tax year. There's no tax to pay on child benefit.

Help for your widow if you don't have dependent children

If your widow is aged less than 60, and you were not receiving (or entitled to) a basic state retirement pension, she can qualify for the lump sum widow's payment.

Chart 9.1: Help from the state for widows and widowers

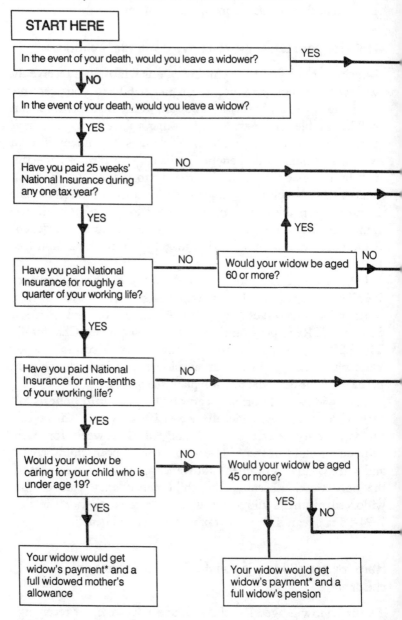

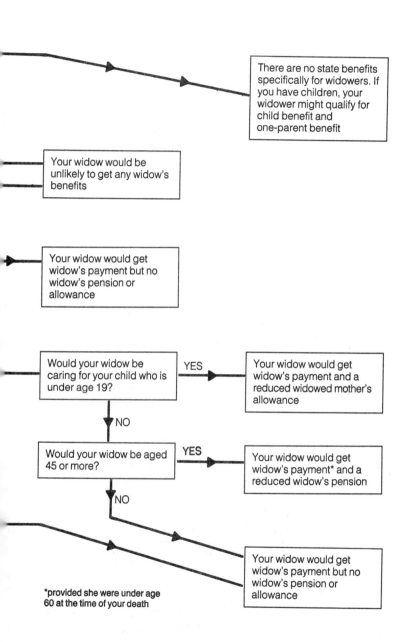

There are no state benefits specifically for widowers. If you have children, your widower might qualify for child benefit and one-parent benefit

Your widow would be unlikely to get any widow's benefits

Your widow would get widow's payment but no widow's pension or allowance

Would your widow be caring for your child who is under age 19?

YES → Your widow would get widow's payment and a reduced widowed mother's allowance

NO

Would your widow be aged 45 or more?

YES → Your widow would get widow's payment* and a reduced widow's pension

NO

*provided she were under age 60 at the time of your death

Your widow would get widow's payment but no widow's pension or allowance

127

If you have no children, or they are all over the age of 18, your widow can't qualify for anything more than the widow's payment unless she is at least 45.

Widows aged 45 or over, without dependent children, can get a widow's pension. This applies to women who are that age when first widowed. It also applies to women who are that age when their youngest, or only, child ceases to be dependent, and thus they cease to qualify for the widowed mother's allowance. Usually, the pension continues to be paid until your widow qualifies for a state retirement pension. But, if she remarries, the widow's pension stops.

The amount of widow's pension varies according to the woman's age at the time she was first widowed. The highest rate is payable to widows who were aged 55 or over. If the woman was younger than this, a lower rate is paid and this lower rate continues to apply year after year. The different rates of widow's pension are shown in Table 9.1 below.

Table 9.1: Amount of widow's pension in the 1993–94 tax year

Age of widow at the time of husband's death [1]	Amount of widow's pension £££ per week
45	17.28
46	21.31
47	25.34
48	29.38
49	33.41
50	37.44
51	41.47
52	45.50
53	49.54
54	53.57
55 or over	57.60

[1] For women widowed before 6 April 1988, the relevant ages are five years younger, with the full rate pension payable for new widows aged 50 or over

Your widow may also be entitled to any SERPS pension you'd built up. The full SERPS pension is payable to widows aged 55 or over. But women who were younger than this when first widowed receive a reduced amount of SERPS pension.

Switching to retirement pension

A widow who is receiving widowed mother's allowance or widow's pension at the time she reaches the normal state pension age of 60 has a choice:

- she can give up the allowance or widow's pension and receive retirement pension instead. The retirement pension will be at least as big as the allowance or widow's pension given up. On top of that, your widow will also receive any SERPS pension she qualifies for in her own right, plus her own graduated pension (if any) and half of your graduated pension (if any)
- she can continue to receive the widowed mother's allowance (as long as she continues to qualify for it) or widow's pension. But at age 65, she will have to switch to retirement pension
- she can give up the widowed mother's allowance or widow's pension *and* not start to receive retirement pension, in order to earn extra pension. This works in the same way as earning extra pension by deferring your retirement pension (see p.36).

The retirement pension your widow receives may be a pension based on her own National Insurance record, or on a mixture of her own and your National Insurance.

What if you hadn't paid enough National Insurance?

Widow's payment is payable at just one rate: if you'd paid enough National Insurance, your widow receives the full amount; if you hadn't paid enough National Insurance, she gets nothing.

Widowed mother's allowance and widow's pension are based on the National Insurance you'd paid during your working life (see p.46). If you hadn't paid enough for your widow to receive the full rate of allowance or pension, she may instead receive a reduced-rate allowance or pension. She should get at least some pension or allowance as long as you've paid National Insurance for a quarter of your working life.

What the state provides for widowers

There are no formal state benefits for widowers and, if you have no dependent children, your widower will usually get no help at all from the state. If you have children under the age of 19, your widower can claim child benefit (see p.125) and he may also qualify for **one parent benefit**. This is available to single parents bringing up one or more child on their own. The child must live with the parent – not just be supported by him. The benefit is usually payable as long as the parent is entitled to claim child benefit, but payment will stop if your widower remarries (or cohabits as if he were married).

In the 1994–95 tax year, one parent benefit is paid at a single rate of £6.15 a week (even if you have more than one child). It is usually increased each year in line with the Retail Prices Index. There's no income tax to pay on one parent benefit. Chart 9.1 on pp.126 and 127 summarises the help available from the state for widowers.

Other help from the state

Widows and widowers on low incomes may qualify for **non-contributory benefits**, such as **income support** and **housing benefit**. These benefits are outside the scope of this book. You can find out about them by contacting your local Benefits Agency (see p.41).

Help from your employer before retirement

If you belong to an employer pension scheme, your dependants will almost certainly be entitled to benefits which are payable in the event of your death before retirement. These will usually take the form of:

- lump sum life insurance
- often a refund of your contributions to the pension scheme
- a pension for your widow or widower, and
- possibly pensions for your children or other dependants.

Some employers have schemes to provide some or all of these benefits even for employees who are not covered by a pension scheme run by the employer.

How much as a lump sum?

The taxman gives tax relief on the amount of money paid in and invested to provide life cover, so naturally enough the taxman also sets limits on the amount of cover which can be provided in this way.

The general rule is that the maximum lump sum which can be paid out in the event of death must not be greater than four times the employee's **final pay**, which is, broadly, pay just before, or near, the time of death. For people covered by the 'post-1989 regime' for employer pensions (see p.69), i.e.:

- people who belong to a scheme which was set up on or after 14 March 1989
- people who belong to a scheme set up before 14 March 1989 but who joined it on or after 1 June 1989
- people who belong to a scheme set up before 14 March 1989 and who joined it before 1 June 1989 but who have chosen to be covered by the 'post-1989 regime' rules

there is also an overall cash limit on the amount of life cover. In the 1994–95 tax year, this limit is £307,200. This cash limit is usually increased each year in line with the Retail Prices Index. Life insurance payable from previous pension schemes and plans that you had counts towards the Inland Revenue maximum, unless the current scheme provides a lump sum of no more than twice your final pay, in which case life insurance from previous arrangements can be ignored.

The tax rules also allow the amount of your (but not your employer's) contributions to the pension scheme to be paid out as a lump sum, in addition to the main amount of cover described above. In some cases, interest is added to the repayment of contributions.

The employer scheme can set its own limit, which may be lower than those set by the Inland Revenue. In this case, you could make additional voluntary contributions (AVCs) – see p.76 – and use them to increase the amount of life cover you get under the scheme. Since you get tax relief at your top rate of income tax on AVCs, this is a very tax-efficient way of buying life insurance.

In most schemes, the scheme trustees (see p.152) have the right to decide who will receive the lump sum in the event of your death. (This enables the scheme administrator to make a payment quickly, without having to wait for probate. It also prevents the lump sum being counted as part of your estate for inheritance tax purposes.) In practice, the scheme will usually pay the money to whomever you have requested – though it would probably override your wishes if you'd failed to name someone – your young child, say – who had been genuinely dependent on you. You should review your request whenever your circumstances change – say, on marriage, or the birth of a child.

How much widow's or widower's pension?

The taxman also limits the amount that can be paid out in pensions to a widow or widower and other dependants. The general rule is that a widow's or widower's pension must not be greater than two-thirds of the *maximum* pension that the employee could have had. 'Maximum' means the maximum according to the tax rules – in other words, based on the taxman's definition of final pay and the number of years that the employee could have been in the scheme (or in that employment) had he remained in the scheme until normal retirement. If you are covered by the 'post-1989 regime' there is also an overall cash limit on the widow's or widower's pension. The limit is two-thirds of £51,200 for the 1994–95 tax year; the limit is usually increased each year in line with the Retail Prices Index. Table 9.2 gives a guide to the maximum pension your widow or widower could receive depending on your pay.

The Inland Revenue's limit usually applies to the sum of benefits from all schemes or plans to which you had belonged. So widow's or widower's pensions payable from schemes which you had belonged to in the past must generally be taken into account when working out the most that your current scheme could pay.

Once the upper limit on the widow's or widower's pension has been found, it can be increased yearly in line with the Retail Prices Index. This provides a ceiling within which the actual pension must remain. Most schemes increase widow's or widower's

Table 9.2: The maximum widow's or widower's pension from an employer scheme [1]

Your earnings from the employer £££ per year	Maximum widow's or widower's pension £££ per year
10,000	4,444
15,000	6,667
20,000	8,889
25,000	11,111
30,000	13,333
40,000	17,778
50,000	22,222
60,000	26,667
70,000	31,111
80,000	35,556 [2]

[1] If you joined the pension scheme on or after 17 March 1987, you must have been able to work for the employer for 20 years up to the time you would normally have retired for the maximum widow's pension to be payable. If you joined before 17 March 1987, 10 years' service is sufficient
[2] Or £34,133 in the 1994–95 tax year if you're covered by the 'post-1989 regime'

pensions by less than the maximum that tax rules allow.

If you were contracted out through your employer pension scheme and it was a final pay scheme, your widow's pension must include a guaranteed minimum pension (GMP) (see pp. 98–99) of at least half the amount of GMP you had built up, provided your widow is 45 or over, or has dependent children. There are special rules concerning increases to GMPs once they have started to be paid (see p. 103).

If you were contracted out through an employer money purchase scheme, the whole of your protected rights 'fund' must be converted into pension for your widow if you're a man, or widower if you're a woman.

A scheme can set its own limit on the pension it will pay provided it doesn't break the taxman's limit. The scheme rules will also determine whether a widow's or widower's pension is payable for life – usually it is. But some schemes either stop paying, or review the position, if the widow or widower remarries.

Pension for other dependants

In the event of your death before retirement, your employer pension scheme can provide a pension for one or more dependants other than your widow or widower. Any one pension can't be more than two-thirds of the maximum retirement pension you could have had – this is the same as the limit applied to the widow's or widower's pension (see p.132).

Furthermore, all the dependants' pensions – whether for your widow or widower, a child or children or some other dependant, such as an elderly relative – when added together must not come to more than the maximum amount which could have been paid to you as retirement pension.

A pension for a dependent child must cease when the child stops being dependent – for example, when the child reaches age 19, or when he or she finishes full-time eduction. Pensions for other dependants can continue for the rest of their lives, even if they cease to be dependent in the literal sense of the word.

Help from your employer after retirement

An employer pension scheme may also provide help for dependants in the event of your death after retirement. This can take a number of forms:

- a separate widow's or widower's pension
- pension for other dependants
- guaranteed payments of your own pension for a set number of years, if you die within that time
- possibly, a lump sum.

How much widow's or widower's pension?

As with pensions payable on death before retirement, the Inland Revenue limits the maximum pension that can be automatically provided for a widow or widower. The limit is two-thirds of the *maximum* retirement pension to which you could have been entitled. 'Maximum' relates to the taxman's definition of final pay, though the calculation is based on the *actual* number of years you have worked for your employer. Once it starts to be paid, the widow's or widower's pension can be increased as long as it does not exceed the maximum possible pension increased in line with changes in the Retail Prices Index.

If you're contracted out of SERPS through a final pay scheme, the scheme must provide a widow's pension of at least half the GMP (see pp.98–99) that you have built up. Since 6 April 1988, there must also have been provision for a GMP to be paid to widowers, provided you were receiving a state basic pension and your husband is getting either a basic pension or a state invalidity pension. There are special rules concerning increases in GMPs once they start to be paid (see p.103).

If you're contracted out through a money purchase scheme, the protected rights must include a widow's or widower's pension of half the amount you had been getting in protected rights retirement pension. The scheme can set its own limit on the widow's or widower's pension, and one-half of the employee's retirement pension is commonly used in final pay schemes. In the majority of schemes, the widow's or widower's pension is based on the employee's potential retirement pension *before* any deduction is made to take account of the employee taking a tax-free lump sum (see p.66).

Most large schemes pay the widow's or widower's pension for life, though some stop the pension, or review it, if the widow or widower remarries. With some schemes, you can increase the pension that your widow or widower would get by giving up part of your retirement pension – you make this decision at the time you retire. The total widow's pension (including any amount provided automatically under the scheme) must not come to more than your remaining retirement pension.

A further point to note is that the GMP is payable to a widow or widower regardless of whether the marriage took place before or after retirement. However, most employer schemes provide non-GMP pensions only for a widow or widower to whom you were married *at the time you retired* – it is not usually possible to add this benefit later if you marry after retirement.

Pensions for other dependants

The scheme can provide pensions for other dependants, such as children or elderly relatives. No one pension can exceed two-thirds of the maximum retirement pension you could have had; and all dependants' pensions (including a widow's or widower's pension) must not, in total, come to more than the full amount of retirement pension you could have had.

Children's pensions are payable only until they cease to be dependent – say, on reaching age 18 or ceasing full-time education. Other dependants' pensions can be payable for life.

Guaranteed payment of your own pension

Your retirement pension is, of course, payable throughout your life, but it would not necessarily stop if you died soon after retirement. An employer pension scheme, in theory, can *guarantee* to pay your retirement pension for up to 10 years, in case your death occurs before that time is up. In practice, other rules make a 10-year guarantee impractical for most schemes. But a five-year guarantee is both practical and in use in many employer schemes.

Usually, the scheme has the right to decide who should receive your pension if, after your death, it continues to be paid for the rest of a guarantee period. But, in practice, your request will usually be respected. Often, the guaranteed pension is 'rolled up' and paid immediately as a lump sum (see below). If your widow or widower is to receive periodic payments of the guaranteed pension, it will usually be paid alongside any dependant's pension he or she receives.

A lump sum

If you retire at the normal retirement date for your scheme, your employer usually won't provide you with life cover after retirement. However, if your death occurred relatively soon after retirement, the scheme might pay out a lump sum if the payment of your pension had been guaranteed (as described above), or if you'd received less in pension than the amount you'd contributed to the scheme over the years. Such a lump sum payment is generally paid free of tax.

Help through a personal pension plan before retirement

A personal pension plan can be used to provide:

- a pension for your widow or widower
- a pension for your children or other dependants
- a lump sum from your pension plan
- lump sum life cover through a related term insurance policy.

With the exception of contracted-out plans (see below), you can choose whether or not to include benefits to be paid in the event of death. The more benefits you decide to include, the less of your fund will be available to provide your retirement pension. But, if you have dependants, it's important that you make provision for them, and using a pension plan can be one of the most tax-efficient ways of doing this.

How much pension for your dependants?

A contracted-out personal plan (see Chapter 7) *must* allow for a widow's or widower's pension to be payable if your widow or widower is aged 45 or over, or is younger than 45 but qualifies for child benefit – these conditions tie in with the widow's benefits available from the State (see p.124). The pension would be whatever amount can be bought by the fund built up through investing the contracting-out rebates (together with tax relief and incentive payments, if applicable). Your widow or widower has an **open market option** which gives her or him the right to shop around for a different pension provider rather than stay with the original plan provider.

The pension *may* cease if your widow or widower remarries while under the state pension age, or ceases to be eligible for child benefit and is still under the age of 45 – but this depends on the terms of the contract at the time of death; it may provide for continued payment of the pension in these circumstances.

A contracted-out widow's or widower's pension must be increased each year in line with inflation up to a maximum of three per cent a year. If you have no widow or widower, the fund built up by the invested rebates can be paid to another dependant or, failing that, paid to your estate, or to someone you nominate.

With personal plans, other than contracted-out plans (or the contracted-out element of a plan), you can arrange for a pension to be paid to your widow, widower, children and/or other dependants in the event of death. With an old-style plan, the amount of money that has built up in your fund is the only limit on the size of the pension, or pensions, that can be paid. With a new-style plan, there is also a restriction that the total of pensions for dependants must not come to more than the amount of retirement pension which your fund could have bought if you could have retired at the time of death.

How much of a lump sum?

If your plan doesn't include any arrangements for paying pensions to dependants, or if you have no dependants, a lump sum can be paid from your plan. With an old-style scheme, this is the amount of your accumulated fund. With a new-style scheme, the lump sum is either the accumulated fund, or could be equal to the return of contributions together with reasonable interest and bonuses. The lump sum doesn't have to be paid to someone who was financially dependent on you.

How much life cover?

You can use up to five per cent of your **net relevant earnings** (see p.88) in premiums for a special life insurance policy used to pay out a lump sum if you die before age 75. You get tax relief at your highest rate on the premiums, but the amount you pay counts towards your overall contribution limit for personal pension plans (see Chapter 6). So, if you want to pay the maximum possible towards your pension, you may do better to arrange separate life insurance outside your personal pension arrangement.

When connected to an old-style personal plan, the life insurance is called a **section 621 policy**. When connected to a new-style plan, it is called a **section 637 policy**. Basically, these two policies are the same. If you're eligible to have a personal pension plan, you can take out a section 621 or section 637 policy on its own, even if you're not currently paying contributions towards a pension.

Help through a personal plan after retirement

With the exception of contracted-out plans, you must choose at the time you start to take your pension which death benefits you want to have as part of your plan. They might include:

- a guarantee that your pension will continue for a set period, in case death occurs within that time
- a pension for your widow or widower
- a pension for other dependants
- the equivalent of any guaranteed pension paid as a lump sum.

Pension guarantee

You can arrange for your retirement pension to carry on being paid for a set period after the date of your retirement, in case your death occurs within that time. The guarantee period can't be longer than ten years. You can nominate the person who will receive your pension if you die within the period – or the lump sum equivalent of it. The recipient doesn't have to be financially dependent on you.

How much pension for your dependants?

A contracted-out personal plan must allow for a widow's or widower's pension as described on p.137. The sum of any pensions for your widow, widower and/or other dependants from a plan which is not contracted out must not come to more than the amount of pension that you were receiving. Otherwise, there is no limit on the amount of these pensions.

CHAPTER 10

Early retirement

FOR MANY people, the idea of early retirement is attractive. But you'll usually have to rely on a smaller pension than you'd otherwise have had. You need to plan ahead if you're to be able to afford to give up work early. But, if ill health forces you to retire early, your pension may be protected to some extent – it depends on the particular rules of your pension scheme or plan.

The state scheme

Choosing early retirement

You can't receive a state retirement pension earlier than the state pension age. Currently, this is 65 for men and 60 for women, but will be 65 for everyone from 2020 (see p.40). Your plans for early retirement will need to take account of this: if you retire before state pension age, you may need income from another source to make up for the lack of state pension; once you are 65 or 60 (whichever applies to you) your income may increase as your state pension starts.

You'll also need to consider whether to continue paying National Insurance after you retire – if you stop, your National Insurance record might not be sufficient for you to qualify for a full state basic pension (see Chapter 3).

Retiring due to ill health

Even if you have to give up work because of ill health or disability, you can't receive the state basic, or graduated, retirement pension early. However, you might qualify for some other help from the state.

If you're temporarily ill, you may qualify for **statutory sick pay** paid by your employer if you're an employee, or **state sickness benefit** if you're self-employed or not working. If you're still unwell after 28 weeks and you've paid the appropriate National Insurance while you were working, you'll be transferred to the longer-term state **invalidity benefit**. This can be made up of a number of parts:

- **invalidity pension** this is the basic invalidity benefit. It's a weekly payment equal to the amount of the state basic retirement pension – £57.60 in the 1994–95 tax year. You get extra if you have dependants, such as a wife and children

- **additional invalidity pension** This is an earnings-related addition to the basic invalidity pension. It's based on your earnings above the lower earnings limit on which you've paid Class 1 National Insurance (in a similar manner to your SERPS entitlement – see Chapter 4). The government is phasing out this part of invalidity benefit, and no *new* entitlements can be built up from 6 April 1991 onwards. Additional invalidity pension in respect of entitlement built up before that date will continue to be payable

- **invalidity allowance** This is an extra payment that you can get if you were under the age of 60 (men) or 55 (women) when your illness started. There are three rates – which one you get depends on your age at the start of the illness (see Table 10.1 below).

Table 10.1: Rates of invalidity allowance in the 1994–95 tax year

Age at the start of your illness		Weekly allowance
Men	*Women*	£
Under 40	Under 40	12.15
40–49	40–49	7.60
50–59	50–54	3.80

Invalidity allowance is reduced by the amount of any additional invalidity pension that you get.

If your illness or disability continues until you reach state pension age, you'll usually stop getting invalidity benefit and receive your retirement pension instead. If you put off the start of your retirement pension, you can carry on getting invalidity benefit but the invalidity pension will be paid only at whatever rate of state basic pension you'd otherwise be getting; in other words, if you'd be getting a reduced-rate basic pension, your invalidity pension will be reduced to that level once you reach state pension age. (But, if you're unable to work because of an industrial injury or an industrial disease, your invalidity benefit won't be reduced in this way.) At age 70 (men) or 65 (women, under the current rules), you have to switch to retirement pension.

If you're receiving invalidity benefit, deferring the start of your state retirement pension won't earn you extra pension. But, it will often be worthwhile delaying the switch to retirement pension because invalidity benefit is not taxable, whereas the retirement pension counts as income for tax purposes.

If you continue to receive additional invalidity pension and/or invalidity allowance after state pension age, it will be reduced by the amount of any GMPs or equivalent pensions that you get from employer pension schemes or personal plans (see pp. 98–103).

From April 1995, sickness benefit and invalidity benefit are due to be replaced by a single new scheme called **incapacity benefit**. There will be three tiers of payment covering the first 28 weeks of illness or disability, the next 24 weeks, and over 52 weeks. The new benefit will be taxable.

There are a number of other state benefits which you might qualify for if you have to retire early because of ill health. They are not covered in this book; you can get details from your local Benefits Agency (see p. 41).

Employer pension schemes

Choosing to retire early

For schemes set up before 14 March 1989, the tax rules normally prohibit an employer pension scheme from paying you a full pension before the normal retirement age for the scheme. For these schemes, the earliest normal retirement age allowed by the Inland Revenue is either 55 or 60, depending on when the scheme was set up or when you joined it (see Chapter 5). But, in practice, most schemes set their normal retirement age later than this. In the past, it was common for schemes to adopt the same ages as for the state scheme – i.e. 60 for women and 65 for men – but over the last few years there has been a trend towards adopting equal pension ages. The most common age is now 65, second most common is 60. The normal pension age for a scheme will usually match the normal retirement age for your employment (as set out in your contract of employment).

Under the tax rules for most pre-March 1989 schemes, the earliest age at which any pension can start to be paid is 50 for men and 45 for women (provided that the woman is within 10 years of normal retirement age). If you retire voluntarily before the normal age for your scheme, the tax rules say that your pension, and other benefits, must be scaled down:

- **retirement pension**   This must not exceed one-sixtieth of your final pay for each year that you've worked for the employer *or* the maximum pension can be set by the following formula if this gives a higher amount: your actual years with the employer divided by the number of years (up to a maximum of 40) that you'd have had if you'd stayed until the normal retirement age, multiplied by the maximum pension you could have had based on your final pay now and the years you'd have been with the employer if you'd stayed until retirement. The maximum pension will be reduced in line with any tax-free lump sum taken up
- **tax-free lump sum**   Similarly, this is also limited. It must not normally exceed three-eightieths of your final pay for each year you've worked for the employer. But, if it gives a higher amount, it can equal the lump sum you would have got if you'd stayed until normal retirement age (though based on final pay now) scaled down by your actual years of service divided by the number of years (up to 40) to retirement age.

Where the pension and lump sum are worked out by the second method outlined in each case above, the limits will be reduced by the amount of any pension from a previous employer scheme or from a personal plan.

For schemes and people covered by the 'post-1989 regime' (see p.69), new Inland Revenue rules apply to pensions which are paid early. As long as you've reached age 50 at the time you start your early retirement, the rules don't require any reduction in your pension, regardless of the normal retirement age for your scheme. In other words, you can receive the full pension your scheme allows – or even the full pension that the Inland Revenue limits, detailed on pp.68 to 72, allow.

The Inland Revenue rules, however, merely set a ceiling on benefits. In practice, most schemes pay less generous pensions, and other benefits, in the case of people who choose early retirement. In particular, the scheme is likely to make a reduction to reflect the fact that the pension will probably be paid for a longer period than a pension starting at the normal retirement age. Employers sometimes offer more generous terms where early retirement is at the request of the employer rather than being your independent decision.

You can start to receive a guaranteed minimum pension (GMP) – see Chapter 7 – from an employer final pay scheme before you reach the state pension age, provided that the pension you receive is not reduced below the amount which must be paid from age 65 (men) or 60 (women). If the pension you would get is less than the GMP due from the state pension age, you can't start taking your pension early.

You can't start to receive a protected rights pension from an employer money scheme before you've reached state pension age.

EXAMPLE 10.1

Ken is 55 and considering early retirement. The normal retirement age for the scheme, which was set up nearly 20 years ago, is 65. Ken has been working for the same employer for the last 15 years and his 'final pay' is £40,000. The tax limits on his pension and lump sum, if he retired now, are:

- **pension** The better of $1/60 \times 15 \times £40,000 = £10,000$ and $15/25 \times (40/60 \times £40,000) = £16,000$. Thus, the upper limit on the pension is £16,000 a year (reduced if a lump sum is taken)
- **lump sum** The better of $3/80 \times 15 \times £40,000 = £22,500$ and $15/25 \times 72/80 \times £40,000 = £21,600$. Thus, the maximum lump sum is £22,500.

In practice, the scheme is rather less generous and will provide a maximum pension of only £7,500. Under the scheme rules, part of this can be swapped for a minimum lump sum of £17,500.

Retiring due to ill health

There are no Inland Revenue limits on the age at which you can start to receive your pension if you have to retire through ill health. You don't have to be completely incapable of work to qualify for an ill health pension – your health may be considered sufficiently bad if it prevents you pursuing your normal work, or if it seriously reduces the amount that you can earn. Each employer scheme will usually set its own conditions, which may be more rigorous than the Inland Revenue rules, and the scheme will normally require medical evidence of your condition.

The tax limits on the amount of pension you can receive are much more generous than those which apply to early retirement for other reasons. The pension and other benefits must not be more than the amounts you could have had if you'd carried on working until normal retirement age (see Chapter 5) but based on your final pay at the time you have to give up work.

An employer scheme will usually set its own limits on the level of ill health pension and related benefits, which may restrict the amounts to less than the maximum allowed by the Inland Revenue.

The rules regarding GMPs and protected rights pensions from employers' schemes (see p.98 onwards) also apply in the case of retirement due to ill health.

EXAMPLE 10.2

If Ken (see example on p.144) were about to retire because of ill health, the maximum pension and lump sum he could have would be:

- **pension** $^{40}/_{60} \times$ £40,000 = £26,667 a year (reduced if a lump sum is taken)
- **lump sum** $^{120}/_{80} \times$ £40,000 = £60,000.

In practice, the scheme sets the benefits below the tax limits. It would pay an ill health pension of £16,667. Under the scheme rules, part of this could be given up for a maximum lump sum of £38,000.

If you were severely ill, and not expected to live for long, the whole of the pension could be converted into a lump sum. There would be a tax charge at a rate of 20 per cent on the part which could not already be taken as a tax-free lump sum. With a small self-administered scheme (see p.77) the Inland Revenue would need to see medical evidence before payment of the lump sum could be approved.

Personal pension plans

Choosing to retire early

With a new-style personal pension plan, you can't normally choose a pension age of less than 50. With the old-style plans, the earliest age is usually 60; but there's nothing to stop you transferring from an old-style plan to a new-style one and then starting your pension before age 60 (though the rest of the new-style plan rules will then apply too – see Chapter 6).

There are no tax rules restricting the pension which you can have in the event of early retirement. But the pension you'll get will generally be lower than a pension which starts to be paid later, because:

- you'll have paid less in contributions
- your investment will have had less time to grow
- your pension will probably be paid for a longer period.

In addition, the plan provider may impose a 'surrender penalty' if you start taking your pension earlier than you'd originally intended. But many plans don't include this type of surrender penalty, so you should be able to avoid these by carefully shopping around at the time you first take out a plan.

You can swap part of your early retirement pension for a tax-free lump sum, subject to the normal rules (see p.83).

Benefits from a contracted-out personal plan (see Chapter 7) can't be taken before the state pension age of 65 for men or 60 for women, even if you're retiring due to ill health (see below).

Retiring due to ill health

If you have to retire because of ill health, you can start to take a pension from a personal plan at any age. You don't have to be entirely incapable of work but you must be ill to the extent that you're judged incapable of carrying out your normal work, or work of a similar nature for which you're trained or otherwise suited. The plan provider will need medical evidence of your condition.

There are no tax restrictions on the pension you can get. But the problems remain that your pension fund will be smaller because less has been paid in and the investment has had less time to grow, and that your pension will be more expensive because it may have to be paid for longer. There are two 'extras' which can be included in personal pension plans which would help to overcome these problems:

- **waiver of premium benefit** If you're ill for longer than a given period – say, six months – you no longer have to pay the contributions towards your regular payment plan, but the plan continues to grow as if the contributions had been made and invested. Most personal plans offer this benefit, usually as an option
- **permanent disability insurance** If you're expected to be permanently incapable of carrying on your work (or similar

work) because of ill health or disability, this insurance guarantees that your ill health pension from the plan will be at least a minimum amount. Though this benefit is allowed under the rules for personal plans, it is, in practice, seldom, if ever, offered at present.

. With both these options, you would have to pay for them by contributing extra towards the plan. The extra amount paid qualifies for tax relief, in the same way as the rest of your contributions, but eats into your overall contribution limit (see pp.88–91) which means you can put aside less through the plan for retirement. With a new-style personal plan, tax rules prevent more than a quarter of your total contributions being used to provide waiver of premium benefit and permanent disability insurance.

Don't confuse **permanent disability insurance** with **permanent health insurance**. The latter provides you with an income if your earnings stop because of illness, even when the illness is temporary and you're expected to recover from it. Permanent health insurance can't be included within a personal pension plan, and premiums that you pay for permanent health insurance don't qualify for tax relief.

CHAPTER 11

Is your pension safe?

State pensions

THE GOVERNMENT is extremely unlikely to go bust and therefore be unable to pay out pensions owed. However, the present Conservative government does have a history of changing the laws relating to state pensions in ways which cut the amount you can eventually get from the state:

- when the government came to power in 1979, state pensions were being increased each year in line with the better of earnings and price inflation. The Conservatives cut the link with earnings, which tend to increase faster than prices
- in 1988, the government revised the State Earnings Related Pension Scheme (SERPS), cutting the eventual maximum SERPS pension from a quarter of earnings between certain limits to just a fifth
- in 1988, the government also introduced a new form of 'contracting out' (see Chapter 7). Originally, contracting out (on a final pay basis) simply affected who paid part of your pension – you could not get less pension as a result of being contracted out. But, under the new way of contracting out (on a money purchase basis), you risk ending up with a lower pension. The government is currently considering further changes to contracting out on a final pay basis – there is a risk that this type of contracting out will now be abolished, taking away the pension guarantee inherent in it
- women born after 5 April 1950 will now have to wait longer to receive their state pension because women's pension age is being raised from 60 to 65.

During the government's 1993 review of the social security system, there were persistent rumours that it might abandon the universal basic pension and replace it with a means-tested pension payable only to those with incomes below a given level, or encourage people to contract out of the basic pension. But more recent press reports suggest that the government may not go down this road after all. Are other pension cutbacks likely?

Certainly the government is concerned about the future cost of state pensions. They are organised on a pay-as-you-go basis: the pensions being paid now are financed from taxes being paid now. Broadly, the working population now supports pensioners now, and future pensioners will be supported by future workers. Looking ahead to the next century, the number of pensioners is going to increase sharply at the same time as the number of people of working age declines – see Table 11.1. Moreover, the real cost of pensions will increase between then and now because SERPS will have been running long enough to be paying out the full pensions it's intended to provide, although by 2030 the cutback in SERPS will have worked through, so its real cost will fall back again. If future workers are to finance a much higher pension bill, it looks as if they will be paying very high taxes. Thus, the government sees a strong need to attenuate the cost of future state pensions.

Table 11.1 The ratio of workers to pensioners

	Number of people of working age for every one pensioner	
Year	If women's pension age had stayed at 60	Now that women's pension age is being raised to 65
1991	3.3	3.3
2020	2.7	3.3
2030	2.2	2.7
2050	2.1	2.5

In general, changes which the government has made to state pensions have been introduced gradually. If you are close to retirement now, you can probably rely on the present system of state pensions continuing. But, if you are relatively young now, you should take into account the possibility that state pensions may provide less in future than now – making it even more important that you arrange your own private pension savings through employer schemes or personal plans.

Employer pension schemes

The revelation, following the death of Robert Maxwell in November 1991, that he had stolen £440 million from the pension funds of his employees and that much of the money might never be recovered, inevitably led people to ask: could it happen again, how safe is *my* employer pension? Largely as a result of the Maxwell affair, the government set up the Pension Law Reform Committee (PLRC – also known as the 'Goode Committee' after Professor Roy Goode who chaired it) to identify the shortcomings of the current system of regulation of employer schemes and to recommend improvements. The PLRC published its report in September 1993.

How are employer schemes regulated now?

The system of regulation now is piecemeal, with a variety of different bodies responsible for different aspects of schemes:

- **the Pension Schemes Office (PSO)** – part of the Inland Revenue – must approve an employer scheme if it is to qualify for the tax reliefs described in Chapter 5. An essential requirement for approval is that the assets of the pension scheme are kept quite separate from the employer's business. This separation is usually achieved by setting up a **trust**; in the public sector, it may be achieved by setting up a **statutory scheme** by Act of Parliament. Such schemes apply, for example, to civil servants, teachers, health service workers and local authority employees. (Some statutory schemes work on a pay-as-you-go basis – see opposite – so problems of segregating a fund do not arise)
- **trustees** a trust is a legal arrangement which gives ownership of specified assets to one or more trustees. The trustees must

look after the assets and use them only for the benefit of specified people – the **beneficiaries**. The purpose of the trust, the way in which it must be used and paid out, and any other rules are set out in the **trust deed and rules**. For more about pension scheme trusts and the role of its trustees, see below

- **the Occupational Pensions Board* (OPB)** is responsible for administering many of the various laws which apply to pension schemes, including the regulations applying to contracting out and information to be disclosed to scheme members. Requirements include *inter alia* that pension funds submit audited accounts at regular intervals. The OPB also runs the Pensions Registry (see p.212) and is able to make grants to support bodies such as the Occupational Pensions Advisory Service (see p.201); it also advises the government on a wide range of pensions matters

- **self-regulating bodies** set up under the Financial Services Act. In particular, the Investment Management Regulatory Organisation* (IMRO) oversees the activities of investment managers, including those concerned with pension funds, ensuring that they are suitable companies to take on the business, have adequate solvency and conduct their business in an honest and professional manner. Many pension schemes are invested with and often administered by life insurance companies and these are overseen by another self-regulating body, the Life Assurance and Unit Trust Regulatory Organisation* (LAUTRO). Similarly, some smaller pension schemes are handled by small investment managers under the aegis of the Financial Intermediaries, Managers and Brokers Regulatory Association* (FIMBRA). See p.158 for more about regulation under the Financial Services Act.

The key role of trustees

Trust law did not originally grow up with pension schemes in mind. It was designed mainly to cope with trust funds set up by families to benefit, say, children and other relatives. In the case of pension funds, the employer sets up the trust and usually decides on the initial benefits and rules (which may later be altered and adapted as the rules and law allow). The aim of the pension scheme trust is to provide pensions and other benefits (for example, on the death of a member) for the members of the scheme – the beneficiaries. The beneficiaries include not just the 'active' members (currently working for the employer) but also people receiving pensions already, people who used to work for the employer and have preserved pensions with the scheme, people who may benefit in certain circumstances, such as wives and children, and also the employer, who is usually able to receive money from the scheme if surplus funds have built up.

Assets are handed over to the trust in the form of contributions paid by the employer, contributions from the members if it is a contributory scheme, and possibly money from the government if it is a contracted-out scheme. The assets grow through the addition of investment income and capital growth. The trustees are responsible for investing the assets in such a way that the aims of the trust can be met.

The employer will sometimes be a trustee – and may be the only one. More often there are a number of trustees, including directors and managers of the company, other employees, perhaps past employees who are now pensioners. The trustees are required by law to consider only the interests of the beneficiaries and not to act as representatives of management or staff, but in practice it is very hard for people to segregate these roles fully.

The trustees of a scheme can be organised in a number of different ways:

- **individual trustees** A number of individuals are appointed. They meet as a group to take decisions, and one of them is usually elected as chairman
- **independent trustee** An individual, otherwise unconnected with the company or pension fund, who can be relied upon to bring a totally non-partisan judgement to bear. From 12 November 1990 onwards, if a pension scheme is wound up, the law requires that an independent trustee be appointed; if the employer was the sole trustee of the scheme, the independent trustee will replace him or her; if there is another arrangement, the independent trustee will

work alongside the original trustees but has the power to outvote them over discretionary matters

- **corporate trustee** A special company is formed to take on the role of trustee. Individuals are elected as directors of the company and its Board of Directors takes the decisions. The directors probably have the same responsibilities as they would have if they were individual trustees, but this is a grey area of the law
- **professional trustee** A pension scheme can employ an outside specialist to act as trustee. This might be, for example, a bank or insurance company with a department or subsidiary which specialises in trust work
- **pensioneer trustee** A small self-administered pension scheme (see p.77) must have as its trustee, or as one of its trustees, a professional called a pensioneer trustee. As well as the normal duties of a trustee, a pensioneer trustee has a duty to the Inland Revenue to guard against the pension scheme being used improperly for the benefit of the employer
- **the employer** The employer can be the sole trustee of the scheme. This is unusual with large schemes, but common with small insurance-based schemes.

The trustees may be appointed by the employer, but this need not be so, for example, employee trustees may be elected by staff or nominated by a trade union according to a constitutional basis laid down in the trust deed and rules. More often, though, the employer retains the right to appoint trustees and may simply agree to appoint employees chosen by the staff or union.

Although the trustees are responsible for the running of the pension scheme, they can employ help, and indeed they have a duty to seek specialist help when required. Commonly, trustees will appoint an administrator to handle the day-to-day business of the scheme, an investment manager to advise on investment strategy and handle the detail of the investment of the assets, an actuary to evaluate the assets and liabilities of the scheme and to advise on the necessary contribution levels, a lawyer to advise on legal aspects and an auditor to check the accounts.

As will be clear from above, the trustees of a scheme will often be ordinary people with little or no prior experience of pension schemes. It is now a legal requirement that trustees are given access to a government booklet which outlines the basic principles of pension trusts, and larger schemes will usually offer some initial training for new trustees. Some schemes also arrange 'top-up' training and ensure that their trustees have access to specialist journals which will help them to keep abreast of the changing pensions environment – but, unfortunately, this on-going training is still all too rare.

How did the Maxwell affair happen?

It is clear from the above outline of the present system that the regulation of pension schemes is piecemeal. The Maxwell affair starkly showed how this fragmented system could be exploited by a determined fraudster.

Most of the money which vanished from the Maxwell pension funds did so during 1990 and 1991. By this time, Maxwell had built up a complex business empire of public companies – the largest of which were Maxwell Communications Corporation and Mirror Group Newspapers – and private companies, many based abroad. When the private companies began to face financial problems, money was shifted to them from the public companies and their pension funds. One way this was done was through 'stock lending' – share certificates are lent to share dealers in return for security (often in the form of government Treasury bills) and a fee – but the Maxwell pension funds didn't receive any security for the stocks lent and the stocks were not returned. Other pension fund assets were used illegally as security for loans made to the private companies. When the loans were not repaid, the lenders assumed that they were entitled to keep the assets. On Robert Maxwell's death, his private empire crumbled and the public companies and pension funds which he had pillaged were left short of funds.

Maxwell had been able to move money around his empire largely without the sanction of any colleagues because he had structured the empire to concentrate power in his own hands. For example, the investment management of some £700 million of pension fund assets had been entrusted to Bishopsgate

Investment Management (BIM) – itself a private Maxwell company of which Robert Maxwell was chairman. In-house investment management companies are not uncommon and they must be regulated under the Financial Services Act (see p.158). Moreover, in most cases, the pension scheme trustees would have as much control over an in-house investment manager as they would over an outside firm. But, in the case of the Maxwell affair, regulation failed and the trustees' power had been usurped by Maxwell.

Pension fund accounts must be prepared every year and audited within 12 months. So why didn't problems show up in the accounts for the Maxwell pension funds? The accounts simply didn't appear on time. The last period for which the accounts were audited was the year to April 1990, although the process was not completed until June 1991. The pension fund audit for the year to April 1991 didn't happen because Maxwell had arranged to change the accounting date (a common enough practice where the structure of a corporation is frequently being altered by takeovers and mergers). The new audit period would have been nine months longer, ending in December 1991. The auditors did request interim accounts since the audit period was so long, but they were never prepared.

The government made a repayable grant available to ensure that current Maxwell pensioners would continue to get their pensions while the liquidators of the private companies searched for the missing assets. A trust fund was set up to receive donations to help, and now agreements are being reached with a range of financial institutions for the return of a large portion of the assets. But there will still be a shortfall, some of which may be borne by members who have not yet retired and whose pension expectations can no longer be met in full.

The PLRC recommendations

The PLRC recommended that the present system of regulation be replaced by a much more integrated system. Trust law would still be the basis but this would be backed up by a new Pensions Act to set out the rights and duties of those involved with pension schemes. The Act would also establish a new

Pension Regulator who would have overall responsibility for the security of pension schemes and would replace the OPB. The Regulator would *inter alia* set out a code of practice for pension schemes and have the power and resources to carry out spot checks and investigations. The Regulator would also be accessible to so-called 'whistle blowers' who have reason to believe that something is wrong with a pension scheme but don't necessarily have hard evidence to support their suspicions.

The PLRC proposed that minimum solvency requirements should be imposed on pension funds so that they always have sufficient assets to meet the demands on the scheme if it were to be wound up today. But the PLRC did not see the need for wide-ranging changes regarding the safeguarding of pension scheme assets – for example, it did not recommend that assets be placed in the custody of an organisation independent of the scheme and its investment managers, nor did it suggest the prohibition of stock lending.

The importance of trustees was acknowledged and the PLRC recommended that the scheme members should have the right to appoint up to two-thirds of the trustees of a money purchase scheme, though only a third of the trustees of a final pay scheme. These splits recognise the fact that, in a money purchase scheme, members bear most of the risk and have the greatest interest in the investment of the scheme assets, whereas, in a final pay scheme, it is the employer who has the greatest risk and interest in the investment policy. The PLRC thought that training for trustees should be encouraged but, regrettably, did not go so far as to say that it should be compulsory.

One of the most important recommendations was for the establishment of a compensation scheme to protect scheme members who lose because of fraud, theft or other misappropriation.

The PLRC recommendations covered a large number of other areas too, including a recommendation that members be given more information about their scheme and their benefits from it, including automatic annual benefit statements for active members.

At the time of writing, the government is consulting interested parties over the changes to the law which should be made in the light of the PLRC report.

Personal pension plans

Unlike the regulation of employer schemes, the regulation governing personal pension plans is much more coherent and largely embodied in the Financial Services Act 1986, but this does not mean that the regulation of personal pensions has escaped problems. Selling and operating personal pension plans counts as investment business under the Act and so plan providers and the middlemen who sell these plans (see Chapter 14) must be authorised to carry on their business.

How the Financial Services Act works

The Financial Services Act established a system of self-regulation. This means that, instead of business being registered and monitored by the government, these tasks are carried out by private sector bodies. The job of regulating investment businesses has been given to the Securities and Investments Board★ (SIB). Although SIB does directly regulate some businesses – in particular, many building societies and banks – the bulk of its regulatory duties have been delegated to four **self-regulating organisations (SROs)** and a number of **recognised professional bodies (RPBs)**. These are shown in Chart 11.1.

It is illegal for an investment business to operate without being authorised, and authorisation is achieved by joining SIB, one of the SROs or an RPB. The SIB, SROs and RPBs operate rules and regulations designed to ensure the investment business is sound and operates honestly and professionally.

In the case of plan providers who are life insurers or unit trusts (or the life insurance arms of, say, banks), the marketing and administration side of the business will most often be regulated by LAUTRO★. If the plan provider runs its own salesforce or tied agents, it will be entirely responsible for the activities of the salespeople and agents who do not themselves have to be authorised.

Where plans are sold through independent advisers (who are not attached to a single plan provider), the adviser must be authorised. Usually, this will be achieved through membership of FIMBRA★, but some larger firms are members of IMRO★.

Chart 11.1: Regulation under the Financial Services Act

SECURITIES AND INVESTMENTS BOARD (SIB)
Overall regulator. Directly authorises some
investment businesses. Delegates regulation
to SROs and RPBs.

SELF-REGULATING ORGANISATIONS (SROs)

FINANCIAL INTERMEDIARIES, MANAGERS AND BROKERS REGULATORY ASSOCIATION (FIMBRA) Regulates independent financial advisers who, for the most part, advise individual investors	INVESTMENT MANAGEMENT REGULATORY ORGANISATION (IMRO) Regulates fund managers and institutions which, for the most part, advise corporate investors	LIFE ASSURANCE AND UNIT TRUST REGULATORY ORGANISATION (LAUTRO) Regulates life insurance companies, friendly societies and unit trusts	SECURITIES AND FUTURES AUTHORITY (SFA) Regulates brokers and market makers in the securities markets	RECOGNISED PROFESSIONAL BODIES (RPBs) Professional bodies regulate members whose investment business is 'incidental' to their main business. Covers, for example, accountants, actuaries and solicitors

Plan providers manage the investment of the money paid into
their plans and usually this side of the business will be handled
by members of IMRO (see p.152).

Deposit-based plans (see Chapter 13) do not count as
investments under the Financial Services Act and so fall outside
this regulatory regime. Deposits offered by banks fall within the
banking supervision rules, which are the responsibility of the
Bank of England. Deposits offered by building societies are the
regulatory responsibility of the Building Societies Commission.

Changes on the way?

The system of self-regulation set up by the Financial Services
Act has encountered various problems over its relatively short
life to date. For example:

- it has proved very difficult to stop fraudulent firms from
  setting up as investment advisers and, though the system has
  shown some success in catching the fraudsters, this has often
  been only after investors' money has been lost
- the cost of self-regulation is high and particularly hard for
  small firms to bear
- the regulation of independent advisers by FIMBRA★, and
  salespeople and tied agents by LAUTRO★ has led to

different regulatory regimes for the different types of middlemen, which is confusing for investors.

The most recent problem to hit the newspaper headlines has been the possible mis-selling of up to 400,000 personal pensions to people who may have been better off leaving their pension savings with an employer scheme. A survey commissioned by SIB* found that, in more than nine out of ten cases, salespeople had not followed the proper rules and regulations. That's not to say that all those customers received wrong advice, but some estimates suggest that as many as a quarter of them may have done. SIB is leading an investigation to identify which people have lost out and qualify for compensation. (For more about how pension plans are sold, see Chapter 14.)

There have been calls for an end to self-regulation, with some experts saying that the regime has failed. Others continue to support the self-regulatory system, but recognise that there must be further adjustments to make the system work better. In particular, it has been suggested that there should be a single SRO which would cover all the investments sold directly to consumers and would regulate both independent advisers and other forms of middleman under a single coherent system. The SIB has made it clear that such an SRO would have to prove that it could provide a significantly better degree of regulation than the existing SROs in this area before it would be allowed to take on these responsibilities.

A committee has been established to set up such an SRO called the **Personal Investment Authority (PIA)**. At the time of writing, it had drawn up draft rules and was awaiting recognition by SIB.

CHAPTER 12

WOMEN AND PENSIONS

IN THEORY, the various retirement pension schemes allow women to build up the same pensions as men – and, in some cases (such as the state scheme), even offer a better deal for women. But, in practice, the picture is very different because of women's historic role and family responsibilities. In the past, this often meant that a woman would forgo all thoughts of a career once she married and might not work at all. Even when married women did go out to work, they had the option to pay lower National Insurance contributions and to rely on their husband's contribution record instead of building up their own state pension (see p.163). This was in keeping with the cultural attitudes of the time, which generally cast men in the role of breadwinners and women as inevitable dependants.

Nowadays, it is far more common for married women, or those living with an unmarried partner, to carry on with a job or career, but having children will still disrupt the work pattern of most working mothers. The result is that women tend to have lower earnings than men and tend to be in pensionable work for fewer years during their working lives. Both these factors mean that women are, in general, unable to build up pension entitlements as good as those built up by men.

This picture is borne out by government figures which show that, in 1992, only 38 per cent of women receiving a state pension were doing so based on their own contribution record. Other figures show that, in 1991, only 15 per cent of women reaching state pension age qualified for a *full* basic pension on their own record, compared with 69 per cent of men. Only 28 per cent of women aged 60 had some SERPS pension, compared with 71 per cent of men aged 65. The picture should improve over time because women are more active in the labour market now than they were in the past and far fewer now pay reduced-rate National Insurance (see opposite). Even so, the Fawcett Society, an organisation working for sex equality, estimates that 2.25 million women earn too little to pay National Insurance, which means that they are not building up any entitlement to state pension. Government figures for September 1993 show that there were 10.55 million women in the workforce but that they account for a high proportion of the 5.5 million part-time workers. Low earnings and broken careers will continue to make it hard for a proportion of women to gain independence in retirement.

Women and the state pension

A bargain on the face of it

As discussed in the Appendix to Chapter 3, women born before 6 April 1950 are able to build up a full state basic pension over 39 years as opposed to the 44 years which apply to men (assuming complete working lives of 44 years and 49 years for women and men, respectively). And the state pension age for these women is only 60 compared with 65 for men. This makes the state system a bargain for those women if they have worked throughout their lives because they pay National Insurance contributions for a shorter period but stand to receive a retirement pension for longer – particularly when you also take into account that women have a greater life expectancy than men (see p.10). Even women who will now have to wait until age 65 for their state pension still benefit on average from their longer life expectancy compared with men.

The problem of traditional women's roles

In the past, married women have had a mixed deal from the state. During the larger part of this century, it has been unusual for women to spend their whole lives working. It was assumed that most women would marry and rely on their husbands to provide for them. This attitude was so much part of Britain's culture that, when the modern social security system was established in the late 1940s (following a famous report by William – later Lord – Beveridge in 1942), women were given a different social security status once they married. On the one hand, they were stripped of various social security rights (such as sickness and unemployment benefit) and became subject to rules regarding retirement pensions which made it hard for married women to build up the same pension as men. On the other hand, the system incorporated a pension for a dependent wife (at 60 per cent of the full pension) to be paid on the basis of the husband's National Insurance record and gave married women the option not to pay contributions at all.

The original system has been altered over the years, but remains fundamentally similar. In particular, the dependent wife's pension is still 60 per cent of the full rate payable to a single person. Until 1977, married women (and widows) who were employed could opt to pay a lower rate of Class 1 National Insurance – called the **married women's reduced rate contribution** – and married women (and widows) who were self-employed could still opt not to pay contributions at all. These options were withdrawn from 6 April 1977, but women who were already paying the reduced rate on that date can continue to do so if they meet certain conditions. (See DSS leaflet *NI1 National Insurance for married women* for details.)

An important change for women was the introduction of **Home Responsibilities Protection (HRP)** in 1978. HRP, described on p.33, helps to protect the pension rights of those people – most often women – caring for children or a disabled relative, say. It makes it possible for women who have a career break for family reasons, nevertheless, to build up a full state basic pension based on their own contribution record, thus breaking the dependency on a husband which was assumed in the earlier versions of the state pension system.

Under current rules, HRP can protect a maximum of 19 years for a woman and 24 years for a man (i.e. the minimum number of years on which a full pension could still be based would be 20). Once women's pension age is the same as men's (from

2020), the government intends that HRP will work identically for men and women and protect up to 22 contribution years. From 1999, HRP is also to be extended to protect SERPS entitlement as well as your right to basic pension.

More about the married women's reduced rate contributions

If you're one of the women who is still paying National Insurance at the married women's reduced rate (see previous page), is it worth switching to full-rate contributions instead? In paying at the lower rate, you give up your rights to certain state benefits, including the right to build up your own basic state retirement pension (and you can't belong to SERPS). Instead, you must rely on your husband's National Insurance record. The maximum state basic pension you can receive based on his record is £34.50 in the 1994–95 tax year. If your husband's National Insurance record would qualify him only for a reduced basic pension, then the amount which you receive would also be reduced by the same proportion.

In deciding whether to switch to full-rate National Insurance, you have to weigh up the pension (and other state benefits) you'd gain against the extra National Insurance you'd have to pay. The answer will depend on your own and your husband's circumstances. For many older women the switch would not generally be worthwhile, on pension grounds, because too little time remains to build up a basic pension which would be better than the amount they will get based on their husbands' contributions. However, whatever your age, if you're on a low income, reduced-rate contributions *might not be saving you any money at all* – in fact, you could be paying out *more* in National Insurance than you would at the full rate. If this applies to you, switching to full-rate National Insurance is likely to be a good idea.

The situation arises because, from 1 October 1989 onwards, full rate National Insurance on the first slice of earnings – up to the lower earnings limit – was reduced to 2 per cent if you pay full-rate National Insurance and earn at, or above, that limit. The 2 per cent rate on the first slice is lower than the married women's reduced rate of 3.85 per cent.

On earnings above the lower earnings limit, the full rate of National Insurance is much higher (10 per cent if you're contracted into SERPS and 8.2 per cent if you're contracted out, for the 1994–95 tax year), so, for women on medium or high earnings, paying at the reduced rate will always work out cheaper than paying at the full rate. It's easy to work out the earnings between which you'd pay less National Insurance by switching to the full rate. If you pay National Insurance at the reduced rate and you would otherwise be contracted into SERPS, you will pay more National Insurance than you need if your earnings are more than £57 a week but less than £74.15 a week at 1994–95 rates. If you pay the reduced rate and could otherwise be contracted out of SERPS, you'll pay more than you need if your earnings are more than £57 a week but less than £81.24. So, if your earnings are below £74.15 or £81.24, respectively, you should seriously consider stopping payment at the married women's reduced rate and switching to full-rate National Insurance instead.

Once you switch to the full rate of National Insurance, you can't ever switch back to the reduced rate. Assuming no increase in the main National Insurance contribution rates, the amount of earnings up to which the reduced rate works out as more expensive will rise each year as the lower earnings limit is increased. But, if you expect your earnings to rise faster than that, paying at the reduced rate might save you money at some time in the future, even though it doesn't now. If you think your earnings will rise appreciably, you're back in the position of weighing up the pros and cons of your position. But, if you expect to remain a relatively low earner, you should consider switching to full-rate National Insurance. Your local DSS office can advise you (see p.41) and DSS leaflet NI1 (see p.163) contains details of how to make the switch.

Employer pension schemes

Equality for men and women

Since 7 November 1987, employers have not been able to require women to retire at a different age from men. However, the Sex Discrimination Act 1986, which gave this right to equal *retirement* ages, did not apply to *pension* ages. Only in late 1993 has a long legal saga concerning equal pension benefits, including the same pension age, for men and women been resolved. The main events in the saga have been:

- **EC Directive 86/378** This European directive, which was made in 1986, makes sex discrimination in employer pension schemes illegal from January 1993 onwards. However, there is an exception – different pension ages can continue to be used until the state pension ages are equalised. The directive was to have been implemented in Britain through the Social Security Act 1989 but the relevant terms have not been brought into force after all because the Barber case (see below) has overtaken the Act

- **Article 119 of the Treaty of Rome** Article 119 requires equal pay for men and women. In a court case (Bilka-Kaufhaus) in 1986, it was determined that 'pay' included pension benefits which supplement (rather than simply replace) the state pension scheme – in other words, there must also be equal pensions for men and women. As the Article is directly enforceable regardless of the national laws in the UK, the court's decision suggested that it was not legal for employer schemes to adopt different pension ages for men and women

- **the Barber case** The situation remained confused until, in 1990, a case in the European Court, *Barber v Guardian Royal Exchange*, found in favour of a man who was made redundant at age 52 but denied a pension at that age when one would have been available to a woman of the same age. The judgement confirmed that pensions are pay under Article 119 and basically required that men and women should be treated equally by employer pension schemes from 17 May 1990 onwards. The Barber case, however, raised question marks over what should be interpreted as equal and whether the judgement applied just to benefits built up from 17 May 1990 or extended to benefits built up before that date. Also, it was not clear whether the judgement, which applied to pensions on early retirement, extended to all aspects of employer schemes, though it was thought to do so

- **the Maastricht Treaty**   At a European summit in December 1991, the Maastricht Treaty was adopted, which included a protocol aimed at clarifying one aspect of the position regarding the Barber case. The protocol proposed that, in most cases, the Barber judgement would be effective only regarding pension benefits built up from 17 May 1990 onwards. Unfortunately, the Treaty is not law until ratified by all the member states of the EC and, at the time of writing, had still not been put into effect.

- **the Ten Oever case**   The position was largely clarified in October 1993 by the European Court's judgement in a case, *Ten Oever v Stichting Bedrijfspensioenfonds voor het Glazenwassers en-Schoonmaakbedrijf*. The case concerned Mr Ten Oever who had been denied a widower's pension from his late wife's pension scheme after she had died. He complained that this was discriminatory because a widow would have received a pension. The European Court, in making its judgement, said that Article 119 of the Treaty of Rome applied not just to retirement pensions but also to other benefits from employer pension schemes, such as widows' and widowers' pensions; it also ruled that equality of pension scheme benefits generally applied only in respect of benefits built up since the date of the Barber judgement – i.e. 17 May 1990

- **Neath v Steeper case**   In November 1993, the European court further clarified the issue of equality by saying that employer schemes *are* allowed to take account of the fact that women tend to live longer than men in calculating non-pension benefits such as tax-free lump sums and transfer values. For example, paying women a higher lump sum than men for the same amount of pension given up won't be illegal.

During the unfolding of this saga, it has been clear that employer schemes would from some date be required to give men and women the same pensions from the same pension age. As a result, the vast majority of employer schemes have over the past few years moved to an equal pension age, if this didn't already apply. The most common age is 65, followed by 60, though other ages have also been adopted. The Ten Oever judgement means that your pension from an employer scheme may now be divided into up to three different phases:

- pension built up before 17 May 1990 which can be different for men and women
- pension built up from 17 May 1990 onwards up to the date at which your scheme equalised pension benefits (including pension age). Benefits must be equal possibly at the best of the benefits offered to men and to women – but this point has yet to be clarified by the European court
- pension built up since your scheme equalised benefits. Equal benefits according to the scheme rules apply.

As a result, it will be many decades before men and women receive equal treatment regarding their *whole* pension from an employer scheme.

The rulings of the European court have important implications for the link between employer schemes and the state pension scheme. In particular, it is inevitable that there will be some change to the system of contracting out of the State Earnings Related Pension Scheme. The government is currently considering the options.

Another area in which European legislation has had an impact is to prevent companies from excluding part-time workers from membership of a pension scheme available to other employees. This is an important decision for women as they are more likely than men to be working part-time.

Personal pension plans

Personal pension plans, to a large extent, offer men and women the same deal. The main difference, at present, comes at the time when the pension starts to be paid, when a given sum of money in the pension plan will buy a smaller pension for a woman than for a man of the same age – this reflects the fact that women will, on average, live for longer than men. In the case of a protected rights annuity from a contracted-out personal plan, this form of discrimination has been abandoned – the same pension must be available to men and women of the same age for a given sum (in other words, the same **annuity rate** must be used).

As a woman, you are more likely to face a broken career record than a man, which makes it harder to build up a satisfactory pension through an employer scheme – especially a final pay scheme. A money purchase scheme is likely to be more suitable at some stages of your life, and personal pension plans can be particularly useful because of their flexibility in terms of the timing and size of contributions.

Pensions and divorce

With a third of all marriages ending in divorce, many women who had left pension decisions to their husbands are suddenly faced with the question of whether they will be financially secure in their retirement. Special rules ensure that a divorced woman can qualify for a basic state pension even if her own National Insurance record is insufficient, but there is no simple solution regarding other pensions.

State pension

If your marriage ends in divorce before you reach state pension age and you do not remarry before you reach that age, you can qualify for a basic state pension based on your own and your former husband's contributions record. Similarly, you can use your former husband's record if your marriage ends after you have reached state pension age. The rules are complicated and you can choose between different formulae for calculating the pension, so get advice from your local Benefits Agency (see p.41).

Other pensions

For more than two decades, a variety of legal, pensions and other bodies have been wrestling with the problem of how to treat divorcing men and women when it comes to the pension rights which have been built up during the marriage. There are two broad approaches to the problem. The first identifies women as potential losers when their marriage breaks up. This is particularly the case if:

- the woman must care for children and thus has either no, or relatively low, earnings from which to make her own savings for retirement
- the woman is relatively mature in years and thus has insufficient time left to build up a reasonable pension.

The second approach is less concerned with avoiding hardship and simply asks how can the pension rights be divided fairly.

There is less agreement about how either of these approaches can be put into practice. The structure of employer schemes and personal plans makes it impossible, at present, simply to split pension *rights*. The right to a pension payable at some time in the future depends on a variety of factors, if it is to materialise – for example, will membership of the plan or scheme continue, will the scheme or plan itself continue until retirement? Moreover, pension rights are *personal* and cannot be assigned to someone else, even if the member has no objection to this.

At present, where a divorce case comes to court, the courts are required to take into account any pension rights when deciding how to allocate the assets (excluding pensions) between a divorcing husband and wife. For example, if the husband has substantial pension rights and the wife none, the court might direct that the wife be given a larger share of the non-pension assets in compensation. But where non-pension assets are limited, such an approach might not be possible. And, under current law, there is no guidance to the courts on how to value the pension assets of the couple.

In the absence of any hard and fast rules, the solution adopted in any one case is left to the discretion of the judge (if the divorce settlement is decided in court), who takes pension rights into account along with a host of other factors. Many divorce cases, however, are settled without the active intervention of the courts and whether or not the pension rights are considered along with other shared assets to be apportioned in some way will depend on the couple and their advisers. Valuing pension rights is outside the scope of most solicitors so, if you are getting divorced and your husband (or you) has pension rights, you should seek advice from a pensions specialist (for example, a member of the Society of Pension Consultants* or the Association of Consulting Actuaries*. You'll have to pay for this advice, but it will be money well spent if it avoids financial hardship (and perhaps protracted argument) in the long run.

In 1992, a working group appointed by the Pensions Management Institute (PMI) started a comprehensive investigation into the treatment of pension rights on divorce. In May 1993, it published a report which recommended that:

- where divorce occurs before retirement, the courts should have the power to share pension rights (but not rights to any death benefits) between the divorcing husband and wife and to direct that a transfer value, equal to the relevant share of the rights, be made to the wife or husband to be paid into their own employer pension scheme or plan (or kept in the original scheme if its trustees agree to this)
- where divorce occurs after retirement, the court should be able to order that part of a pension be earmarked and paid to a former wife or husband. To overcome the problem of the earmarked pension ending when the pension scheme member dies, the report suggested that employer scheme trustees should be encouraged to pay a dependant's pension to a former wife or husband on the death of a member, and that the courts should be able to direct that the scheme member take out life insurance in favour of his or her former wife or husband.

The Pension Law Review Committee (see p.151) endorsed the recommendations of the PMI working group and it seems likely that the law will be altered along these lines but, at the time of writing, the government had yet to take any action.

CHAPTER 13

CHOOSING A PERSONAL PENSION PLAN

THERE'S a huge choice of personal pension plan providers and literally hundreds of individual plans to choose from. Here, we outline the features you might want to look out for; in Chapter 14, we look at the nuts and bolts of taking out a plan and getting advice.

How do you want to save?

Most plan providers offer both regular contribution plans and single lump sum contribution plans. Often, you (or you and your employer, if he or she's contributing to your plan) have to invest at least a given amount – for example, £20 a month or £200 a year with a regular contribution plan, or £500 or £1,000 with a single contribution plan. Most regular contribution plans will accept extra one-off payments, though once again there may be a minimum amount for these, such as £250 or £500.

The majority of regular premium plans will let you increase your contributions if you want to. With some plans you can arrange to increase your payments automatically each year by a set amount, or in line with the index of National Average Earnings (which is published by the government).

An important feature to look out for with a regular premium plan is: can you miss one or more payments without penalty? This can be important if you have a temporary hiccup in your earnings or your circumstances change, and can be useful if, say, you want to take a career break. You may need to pay extra for a 'waiver of premium' option which allows you to miss payments if your earnings fall because of illness or redundancy. Most plan providers also offer plans which will accept just the payments from the government, if you want to use a personal plan simply for contracting out of SERPS (see Chapter 7).

Regular payments or lump sum – which is best?

A regular payment plan can be useful in providing an element of discipline in your saving, and in helping you to save a large amount, but in manageable chunks. Regular payment plans will be suitable mainly for people in employment who receive a steady income. At one time, a regular premium plan let you lock into a fixed level of charges, but sadly those days are gone and the plans, these days, give the provider flexibility to increase charges during the life of the plan. So, don't look solely at what you'll be paying now, look also at what you might have to pay in future. Also check what flexibility the plan gives *you* – for example, it can be very useful to be able to make an extra ad hoc payment into the plan if you have a windfall. Equally, it can help to minimise hardship if you're able to miss contributions without penalty, or reduce the amount you pay. Lump sum plans give you far more flexibility since you just take out a plan whenever you want and have funds available. If you run your own business, or you're an employee whose income varies a lot, you may find single premium plans more suitable than regular premium ones. But you'll have to impose your own discipline on your savings habit. Also, you'll have to accept whatever terms apply to each plan when you take it out, so you can't 'lock into' favourable terms in the way that you may be able to do with a regular payment plan.

Overall, you may pay more in charges (see p.178) if you take out a series of lump sum plans than you would have by taking out one regular payment plan. However, regular payment plans will generally penalise you heavily if you stop the plan or transfer it (see Chapter 8) in the early years.

Other things being equal, you may do best by making steady, but possibly modest, contributions to a regular payment plan, but choose one which allows you to make extra one-off payments as and when you can afford them. A generally slightly more costly option would be to have a regular contribution plan as the backbone of your pension saving but take out additional single premium plans when you want to set aside a bit more.

How your money is invested

There are a number of different ways in which the money in your plan can be invested. Some plans *always* invest just one way, others give you a choice. The broad methods of investment are described below.

Choosing your own investments

Plans which let you choose your own investments are called **Self Invested Personal Plans** or **SIPP**s. You build up your own fund of investments comprising assets that you've chosen yourself. Regulations place some limits on your choice but the range is wide and can include UK shares, British Government stocks, and property, among others. In practice, a 'do-it-yourself' pension plan is likely to be uneconomic unless you have a large sum to invest.

Unit-linked plans and unit trusts

Unit-linked plans are offered by many insurance companies. Your money is allocated to units whose value is linked to a specific fund of investments. Unit trusts offer similar plans and your money buys units in a pool of investments. With both, your return depends on the price of your units; this rises and falls in line with the value of the underlying investments.

There are different types of investment funds and unit trusts, investing in, for example, UK shares, foreign shares, British Government stocks, and so on. A managed fund or mixed unit trust invests in a broad spread of different investments. You can usually choose to invest in more than one fund at once, but there may be a minimum investment for each one. Generally, you can switch between the different funds or different trusts after you've started the plan.

With-profits plan

These are offered by insurance companies and a few friendly societies. Your money is invested by the plan provider in a broad spread of investments – shares, British Government stocks, etc. Your return depends largely on how well the investments grow, but also on other factors, such as the provider's profits from other parts of its business, its level of expenses, etc.

Your return is in the form of bonuses: **reversionary bonuses** are added to your plan regularly – often yearly; a **terminal bonus** is usually added at the time you convert your investment fund into pension. Once added, bonuses can't be taken away, so the amount in your plan can never fall. But the level of future bonuses isn't guaranteed. Plan providers are usually cautious about increasing reversionary bonuses, and reluctant to cut them. However, many insurance companies have cut their reversionary bonus rates in recent years. The level of terminal bonus can vary greatly, and can amount to a sizeable proportion of your plan. A survey by *Pensions Management* magazine in 1993 found that the terminal bonus made up nearly half of the return for the top-performing regular premium with-profits plan over 15 years. For the best single premium with-profits plan over the same term, the terminal bonus accounted for nearly 70 per cent of the return.

Unitised with-profits plans

These are a cross between unit-linked and with-profits plans. They are increasingly replacing the traditional with-profits pension plans offered by insurance companies and can either be a separate plan, or an option within a unit-linked plan.

Your money is allocated to units in the with-profits fund. The amount of your capital can't fall, and it can grow in two ways: the value of units is increased throughout each year in line with a declared bonus, or growth, rate – similar to the reversionary bonuses you get under a with-profits plan. Also, a terminal bonus may be added at the time you take your pension.

Deposit-based schemes and funds

Deposit-based schemes can be offered by banks and building societies but seldom, if ever, are. Deposit administration plans, which work basically like deposit accounts, are run by a handful of insurance companies. A cash fund or money market fund as an option within a unit-linked plan is similar. Your money is invested in an account to which interest is added periodically. The amount of your capital can't fall and grows as the interest is added, but the level of future interest rates isn't guaranteed.

Which type of plan?

Your choice of investment depends largely on how much risk you're willing to take, and the length of time to go until you need your pension. In general, to have the chance of a higher return, you'll need to take more risk. Unit-linked plans and unit trusts, where the amount of your investment can fall as well as rise, are more risky than with-profits plans, where your investment increases but can't fall back. Deposit-based schemes and funds are generally viewed as the least risky, since the amount of your capital can't fall, and because interest rates tend to be more steady than the terminal bonus rates on with-profits policies. But the deposit-based schemes and funds will tend to give the lowest returns and are vulnerable to inflation.

It's essential that long-term retirement savings should be invested so that their value at least keeps pace with inflation. If you're a long way from retirement, you should probably be looking mainly at unit-linked and unit trust investments, as these give you the best chance of beating inflation and of getting a good return over the long term. Choosing a managed fund or mixed trust is less risky than going for more specialised funds or trusts. If you prefer a lower risk strategy, or you are within, say, 10 or 15 years of retirement, consider investing part of your money on a unit-linked or unit trust basis and part on a with-profits basis. When you're within a few years of retirement, deposit-based schemes and funds can be a way of protecting your past investment growth from falls in stock market prices.

Charts 13.1 and 13.2 show how various types of pension plan and unit-linked funds have performed over the last five and ten

Chart 13.1: Past performance of personal pension plans over five years[1]

	worst plan ←————————————————→ best plan	
Deposit administration	£5,503 ☐ £6,386	
Cash/deposit unit-linked fund	£4,898 ☐ £6,891	
Traditional with-profits	£5,676 ☐ £7,566	
Unitised with-profits	£5,986 ☐ £7,338	
Managed unit-linked fund	£5,482 ☐ £8,001	
UK equity unit-linked fund	£5,442 ☐ £8,098	

Source: *Financial Adviser* survey, January 1994

[1] Plan for a man rotiring on 1 December 1993 at age 65, having paid regular premiums, before tax relief, of £1,000 a year

Chart 13.2: Past performance of personal pension plans over ten years[1]

	worst plan ←————————————————→ best plan	
Deposit administration	£15,226 ☐ £15,815	
Cash/deposit unit-linked fund	£13,723 ☐ £17,368	
Traditional with-profits	£18,064 ☐ £26,463	
Unitised with-profits	£19,451 ☐ £22,083	
Managed unit-linked fund	£13,692 ☐ £20,855	
UK equity unit-linked fund	£14,740 ☐ £25,224	

Source: *Financial Adviser* survey, January 1994

[1] Plan for a man retiring on 1 December 1993 at age 65, having paid regular premiums, before tax relief, of £1,000 a year

years. The first point to note is that there is a big difference between the best plans and the worst, though, unfortunately, you cannot know in advance which plans will turn out to be best. Among the five-year plans, the worst cash/deposit unit-linked fund did not even return the amount paid in contributions.

The relatively large difference between the best and worst performers for the managed and UK equity unit-linked funds, compared with the with-profits plans and deposit-based plans, reflects the more risky nature of unit-linked funds.

In theory, taking on more risk should give you the chance of a better return. Certainly, the with-profits plans beat the deposit-based plans. Over five years, the best of the unit-linked managed and UK equity funds have beaten the with-profits plans as you might expect, but over the ten-year period, with-profits plans have, on the whole, performed a lot better than the unit-linked funds. This was in part due to very generous bonuses paid during the 1980s which could not be sustained in the long run. Bonus rates have fallen back and future with-profits performance is more likely to echo the pattern in Chart 13.1.

Fees and charges

With deposit-based schemes, the rate of interest offered will reflect the expenses incurred by the plan provider, though sometimes there are separate charges that you must pay too – for example, an administration fee. Similarly, the level of bonuses earned under a with-profits plan incorporates an allowance for expenses – though again you'll usually have to pay a separate policy fee or administration charge as well.

The position with unit-linked plans, unit trusts and unitised with-profits plans is quite different: there are generally few hidden expenses. Instead, you pay a variety of explicit charges. Unit trust charges are relatively simple, but the plans offered by insurance companies often have a very complicated charging structure. Table 13.1 summarises charges you may come across.

Table 13.1: Charges for unit-linked and unit trust plans

Name of the charge	Description
Charges used with both unit-linked and unit trust plans	
Bid-offer spead	The difference between the higher offer price at which you are allocated or buy units and the lower bid price at which you cash them in. Typically, the spread will be around 5 to 6%
Management charge	A yearly charge set against the investment fund or unit trust to cover the costs of managing the underlying investments. Typically, this might be about 1% or 1.ɔ% of the amount of the fund or trust
One-off administration charge	There might be a single charge at the outset of the plan, or deducted from the first year's payments
Additional charges with unit-linked plans	
Policy fee and/or administration charge	A deduction made at regular intervals to cover the costs of the paperwork, etc., involved in setting up and running the plan
Unit allocation	A given percentage of each payment is allocated to units. The percentage may be lower in the earlier years of the plan, and it may be lower if you pay monthly, say, rather than yearly. Don't be misled by allocations of over 100%: it sounds as if you're being credited with more money than you've paid in but this isn't so – it may mean 100% of the money left after a policy fee or administration charge has been deducted, or you may be getting a refund of part of the management fee
Capital units	You may be allocated 'special' units, especially in the first year or two of the plan, which have a much higher management charge – for example 3% or 5% of the amount of the fund. You usually carry on paying this higher charge throughout the life of the plan
Surrender charges	You're likely to be credited with only part of the value of your plan if you stop paying into it, or transfer it, in the early years

Note: unit-linked plans may charge you if you switch your contributions and/or invested money from one fund to another, though the first switch, or two, each year is usually free. Switching unit trusts will be expensive if you have to sell units in one trust and buy units in another. But some unit trust plans make use of 'umbrella funds' – the trust is split into a number of different funds between which you can switch either free or at low cost

Transferring your plan before retirement

You don't have to contribute to the same plan until retirement. You can stop contributing but leave the money which has already built up invested in the plan. Alternatively, you can transfer your money to another personal plan or to an employer pension scheme, if the plan or scheme agrees to accept the transfer.

All personal plans must give you the right to take a transfer, but watch out in case there are penalties for stopping the plan early. These might take the form of surrender charges (see Table 13.1), or you might be losing the right to a 'loyalty' bonus paid only if you continue the plan for a set period or until retirement. Surrender charges are often very severe if you stop or transfer a plan in the early years – the value of your plan may be less than the amount paid in contributions and, if you stop the plan in the first year or so, it may well be worth nothing at all.

When can you retire?

The tax rules normally allow you to take the proceeds of a new-style personal pension plan at any age from 50 to 75. But protected rights from a contracted-out plan (see Chapter 7) can't be taken before state pension age (currently 65 for men and 60 for women). Within these limits, the plan may set its own rules.

With some plans, you have to choose a retirement date at the time you first take out the plan, though there will be no penality if you retire after that date. But there may be a penalty if you retire earlier, so it's probably best to choose the earliest possible date at the outset, even if you subsequently change your mind. Many plans don't insist on a set retirement date, but let you choose near the time.

Retiring at 50 may seem like an attractive option, but in practice it might not be feasible. The size of your pension will depend largely on how much you invest, how the investment grows, and how much pension you can 'buy' with your fund. If you retire early, you'll have invested less, your fund will have had less time to grow, and you'll be using the fund to buy more years of pension. If you plan to retire early, you should be prepared to save more and from an earlier age than if you're aiming for a later retirement.

You don't have to stop work to be able to take a pension from a personal plan. This means that you could ease back on work but maintain your income by starting to take a pension before you fully retire. Having several personal plans with different pension ages adds to your retirement flexibility.

Pension choices

There are different types of pension that you can choose: a level pension, one which increases by a set amount each year, or one which increases in line with price inflation, usually up to a certain limit, such as five per cent a year. Your pension can also be guaranteed to be paid for a certain number of years, in case death occurs within that period. Different plan providers also offer different terms for providing widow's, widower's and children's pensions, if you are the one to die first after the pension has started.

You don't have to make your choice about these features at the time you take out the plan, as long as the plan gives you an **open market option** – all new-style plans used for contracting out must give you this option, and most other plans do too. The open market option allows you to take your fund to another plan provider (which must be an insurance company or friendly society) at the time you want to start taking your pension. So you can leave your shopping around for a pension until then. However, at the time you start the plan, you should check whether there will be any penalty if you exercise your open market option at retirement. For example, a penalty might be in the form of a **retirement bonus** which you get only if you stay with the original plan provider.

Life insurance

If you're eligible to take out a personal pension plan, you're also eligible to take out a special term insurance policy, a **section 621 or 637 policy**. This is a protection-only policy which provides a lump sum or income for your dependants in the event of your death. Unlike other forms of term insurance, you get tax relief at your top rate of tax on the premiums you pay.

You don't have to take out a section 621 or 637 policy with the same company or society that provides your pension plan, and you can take one even if you don't take out a pension plan. For further details about section 621 and 637 policies, see p.139.

Comparing pension plans

Once you've settled on the broad type of plan that you want and the features you need, you'll generally still be left with a choice of different plan providers. Unfortunately, there's no easy way to choose between them.

Plan providers, and most advisers, make much of the past investment performance of particular providers. There's no doubt that investment performance is likely to be the single most important factor in determining how much pension you receive. But, sadly, there is no reliable way of predicting in advance which plan providers will perform best – especially when you're looking at very long-term investments, such as pensions. Many studies have been carried out, in universities and business schools in Britain and in America, which have found no relationship at all between past investment performance and future performance.

Despite the evidence, you're likely to find that the investment track record of a plan provider is the feature which is often stressed more heavily than any other by salespeople and advisers. You'll also find that specialist magazines (see p.184) list investment performance for plan providers. Perhaps a reasonable rule of thumb is to stick to providers whose plans *consistently* perform better than average. Don't be seduced into picking just this year's top performer – next year's results might be entirely different. You should also look at other factors. These might include:

- **financial strength** What reserves does the plan provider have? Reserves are a bit like the 'emergency fund' you probably keep handy in the building society in case times become hard. A plan provider needs sufficient reserves to guard against going bust, and the law specifies minimum reserve levels for the various plan providers. But going bust is an extreme situation. You need to consider financial strength in another light: a provider may be giving its investors good returns now, but can they keep it up? For example, are they dipping into reserves to keep up bonus rates – this is a bit like selling the family silver to pay the gas bill. Is there a risk that investment returns will be cut in future, or that charges will have to be increased?

- **expense levels and charges**   Very few plan providers offer plans with charges that are fixed for the life of the plan. With some plans, there is an upper limit above which charges can't rise, but with many there's no ceiling specified. And, where there are no explicit charges, the expenses which influence the interest rate or bonus rate can usually vary without limit. So it's a good idea to have a look at how efficiently the plan provider manages its business – does it run up high expenses, or are they relatively low?

- **investment philosophy**   Higher-risk investments tend to give higher returns over the long term, but risky investments can go badly wrong. A 'safer' investment strategy may give a steadier return, but the results over the long term may be poorer. What approach does the plan provider take?

- **other factors**   How is the plan provider's business organised – as a company with shareholders to consider and as a source of business capital, or as a mutual organisation owned by its investors? Is it part of a larger group, does it have a foreign parent, to what extent can it draw on the resources of the rest of the group or of the parent company? Is the business growing, static, or declining, is the organisation eager to compete for pensions customers?

It used to be very difficult for the individual to get any information about these sorts of factors. However, insurance companies offering with-profits plans now have to make available much more information of this sort. They must produce a booklet, giving facts and figures about the company's with-profits business, which is available on request.

And all plan providers are now required to publish 'reduction in yield' (RIY) figures which show the overall effect of charges on the return you might get from a plan (see p.198). On the whole, this new information is fairly difficult for the average person to use and interpret; but a good financial adviser (see Chapter 14) should be able to help. You can glean useful information from specialist magazines, such as *Pensions Management* and *Money Management*.

More information

If you're already interested in the plans offered by particular providers, you can get information about the plans direct from them. The telephone book may have the address and phone number of a local branch or office. If not, your local library should be able to find details of the head office for you.

Specialist magazines are a useful source of information about plans generally and of surveys comparing the different plans which are available. An added advantage is that surveys usually give details of how to contact the providers for more information. Some magazines are available through newsagents. With many, you can arrange a subscription, or obtain single copies, direct from the publisher. Specialist magazines which run regular surveys of pension plans include *Money Management* and *Pensions Management*, both published by FT Business Enterprises★. *Which?* magazine also publishes regular articles about personal pensions, including comparative surveys of many of the plans available – see, for example, *Choosing a Pension* in *Which?*, August 1992. Copies of *Which?* are kept by many public reference libraries and details of how to subscribe can be obtained from Consumers' Association★.

CHAPTER 14

SHOPPING FOR A PERSONAL PLAN

YOU CAN buy a personal pension plan either direct from the plan provider or through a middleman. There are three types of middlemen:

- **direct salespeople** – individuals who work for a single plan provider and sell the products of just that provider
- **tied agents** – individuals or firms who are selling the services of just one company. They range from small businesses to giant High Street banks and building societies
- **independent advisers** – these can sell the full range of products available from all the companies in the market. Again, these may be small or large firms. A few High Street banks and building societies operate through their branch networks as independent advisers, rather than as tied agents or outlets for their own insurance subsidiary, but most of the major banks and societies also have a separate independent adviser operation which generally deals only with wealthier clients.

When you first have contact with middlemen, they should tell you whether they are independent or tied, and which regulatory body (see p.158) oversees them. They should also provide you with a buyer's guide, which explains what type of service they can give you.

Before you do business with any plan provider, salesperson, agent or adviser, you should check his or her credentials. All personal pension plans (except the deposit-based plans which can be offered by banks and building societies) count as investments under the Financial Services Act 1986. That Act requires that anyone advising about, or selling, investments must be **authorised** (or directly connected – for example, as employee – to someone else who is authorised). To get authorisation, a firm must be 'fit and proper' to carry on its investment business and must be financially sound. A firm or person which carries on investment business in the UK without authorisation is committing a criminal offence.

An investment business can be authorised directly by the Securities and Investments Board★ (SIB), the official body that oversees the running of the Financial Services Act, or through one of the bodies to which the SIB has delegated some of its powers. These bodies are the four Self-Regulating Organis-ations (SROs) and the Recognised Professional Bodies (RPBs).

If you're considering pension plans that fall within the scope of the Act, you should not have any dealings with a business which is not authorised. If you come across such a business, or are uncertain about its status, you should report it to the SIB.

The SIB keeps a Register of authorised investment businesses. It gives you details of the authorising body, the status of the business, the types of products it deals in and the address of the business. Before you deal with a plan provider or adviser, you should check the entry in the Register: if it is not listed, it is not authorised. Make sure that the Register entry shows that it is authorised for the type of business you propose to do with it.

You can check the SIB Register by writing to the Information Office, SIB, or by telephoning a special number for Register enquiries: 071-929 3652. Alternatively, you can consult the Register directly using **Prestel** – an electronic information system available in most main libraries; library staff will help you use it.

Dealing with a plan provider or a salesperson

Getting in touch

You might decide to deal directly with the plan provider if, say, you've been satisfied doing business with it before, or if you've picked it out from a published survey of the market (see p.184).

You might get in touch with a company direct in response to an advertisement in the press.

Literature from the company will give you an address and phone number you can contact. A published survey will often include contact details. Otherwise, you may find the address of a local branch in the telephone book. Failing all these, most public libraries have business directories in their reference section which will give you the details of the head office.

It's a good idea to get details from two or three plan providers at this stage, so that you can compare them in detail, fully check what the plans offer, their charges and so on, and select the most suitable one for you. The plan provider will usually arrange a meeting with one of its salespeople either at its premises, or at your home, but if you would prefer to study the plan in private, just ask the provider to send you all the relevant literature.

The selling process

In the case of pension plans from life insurance companies, friendly societies and unit trusts, there are regulations under the Financial Services Act 1986 which are aimed at protecting you from bad or dishonest selling practices. One of the most important regulations is the 'know your customer' rule: the salesperson must gather enough information about you and your circumstances to put him or her in a position to assess your needs and to decide whether or not the products he or she has to sell are suitable for you. If you're looking at pension plans, the adviser should – as a minimum – find out about the following:

- your age and sex
- your employment status
- your earnings and other sources of income
- your tax position
- your state of health
- whether you have a husband or wife
- whether you have children, and their ages
- your regular financial commitments (such as mortgage payments, household bills, and so on) and your likely commitments in retirement

- your intended retirement age
- your likely entitlement to state pensions
- details of any employer pension scheme that is open to you
- details of any previous employer schemes from which you're entitled to a pension at retirement
- details of any personal plans that you have
- details of any life insurance you currently have
- details of any other savings and investments
- how much you can afford to pay into a pension plan
- whether you want to transfer any funds from previous pension schemes or plans into a new plan
- what features you want your plan to have
- your attitude towards investment risk
- likely changes to any of the above.

The only situation in which less information would be sufficient is where your intention is only to contract out of SERPS through a rebate–only plan (see Chapter 7). In this case, the plan provider needs to know your age and sex, employment status, earnings, details of any employer scheme open to you, and your attitude towards investment risk.

Once the salesperson has got to know you, he or she must recommend to you the most suitable of the company's wares or, if none is suitable, he or she must tell you so. He or she should help you to make your decision in the light of the options open to you, so, for example, if you could join an excellent employer scheme and it would be unlikely that a personal plan could beat it, the salesperson should tell you that none of his or her products is suitable for you. In practice, the position is not so clear cut: though there are strict regulations about how the benefits from a personal plan are to be estimated (see p.197), there are no corresponding rules for illustrating the benefits from employer schemes. If the salesperson tends towards a pessimistic attitude to your employer scheme, a personal plan could look more attractive than it would appear given different assumptions. Similarly, if you are interested in contracting out of SERPS, the assumptions the salesperson must use to show you the possible benefits from a rebate–only plan are entirely different to those used by the DSS to estimate your

SERPS pension (see p.56). Misleadingly, this places the rebate-only plans in a better light vis-à-vis SERPS than is justified.

A salesperson for one company within a group of related companies might be unable to sell the full range of that group's products. If he or she recognises that the product of another company within the group might be suitable, he or she can offer to arrange for you to meet with the salesperson for that other company. For example, a life insurance salesperson might arrange contact with the unit trust arm of the same group.

A salesperson for one company can't recommend the products of another company. In the rather unlikely event that, on your own initiative, you asked the salesperson to arrange for you to buy the products of an entirely different company, the salesperson could do this on what's called an **execution-only** basis – he or she would act merely as a channel for your business, but could not advise or comment on it.

When you have agreed to a deal, you'll be given or sent detailed information about the product. You'll also receive a **cancellation notice** which tells you that you have the right to withdraw from the deal within 14 days of receiving the notice. After 14 days, you're committed to the contract.

The Financial Services Act does not apply to deposit-type personal pension plans, such as those which can be offered by building societies. They are covered by regulations overseen by the Department of Social Security, but these are scant compared with the Financial Services Act.

Doorstep selling

You might also find yourself in contact with a salesperson as the result of a **cold call**. This is when a salesperson telephones, or appears on your doorstep, out of the blue. Personal pension plans offered by life insurance companies, friendly societies and unit trusts can be sold in this way. There are strict regulations which apply to such calls, including:

- the salesperson should introduce himself or herself, make clear the company represented, provide you with a buyer's guide and ensure that you understand that he or she is unable to sell the products of any other company. If the call is a

personal visit, he or she should give you a business card
- the salesperson should make clear the reason for the visit, and establish whether or not you wish the call to continue. If you don't, he or she must respect your wishes and end the call
- he or she must respect your right to end the call at any time
- if, at the time of the call, you agree to invest in a product, you must be sent subsequently a cancellation notice (see p.189) which gives 14 days to back out of the deal.

Despite the regulations, a cold call can be an unwelcome, and even distressing, intrusion. The salesperson is there in the hope of making a sale and will have been trained in all sorts of persuasive techniques, so you're right to be wary. You should bear in mind the following points:

- if you're not interested in the products, don't be afraid to end the call – as a last resort, you can simply hang up the telephone or close the door
- if you are interested, but would prefer to consider the product in peace and in your own time, ask the salesperson to give you, or to post to you, the relevant literature, and say you'll be in touch if you want to pursue the matter further. If he or she won't agree, hang up or close the door
- if you're interested and want the call to continue, invite the salesperson in, but remember that however friendly, this is basically someone who wants your business. The salesperson is not your guest, and if he or she becomes too persistent you will have to be inhospitable
- if you like the product, don't sign up there and then. It may be the best product for you, but you can't be sure until you've compared it with other products. Also, you should pause to make sure that you really want it, and that you can afford it. It's best to ignore the temptation of discounts and free gifts if you sign straightaway. You could pay dearly in the long run for a hasty decision made now, particularly with a long-term investment such as a pension plan
- if you do agree to a deal at the time of the call, remember that you have a cooling-off period within which you can change your mind. Make use of that period to check that the product really is one that you want.

Going to a tied agent

Getting in touch

You'll see tied agents' advertisements in, say, local newspapers, trade directories and the *Yellow Pages*. Often, a tied agent will make initial contact through a cold call (see p.189) or by posting literature to you. You may be on an agent's mailing list as a result of having shown interest in other of their products, or you may be on a mailing list which the agent has bought from an outside source. You'll also find tied agents in your high street. Most banks and building societies are tied agents. Other such agents include small firms operating under a variety of names, such as 'insurance and pensions adviser', 'insurance consultant', 'pensions consultant', 'financial adviser'

The selling process

The Financial Services Act prohibits a middleman from advising on and selling the products of a handful of companies; the middleman must either sell the wares of *one* company or deal in the full range of products on the market. This regulation was made to stop the misleading, and previously fairly common, practice of an investment adviser appearing to give independent advice about the whole market when in reality he or she was channelling all the business to just a few companies. A tied agent is now *always* marketing the wares of just one company.

Unfortunately, there's no requirement for tied agents to display their status on their shopfronts, so you might not be aware of it until you're inside. If you don't want tied advice, or don't want to invest in the products of the particular company to whom the agent is tied, don't be afraid to leave.

The status of bank and building society branches can be particularly confusing. A few building societies have their own pension products, but most societies sell the pension plans of others – usually insurance companies. A few building societies act as independent advisers, but most are tied to a single plan provider. The position of the banks is similar; the main difference is that some of the bigger banks have their own insurance company arm whose products they sell through their branches. But to complicate matters, some banks and building societies give tied advice through their branches, but also have a separate operation which gives independent advice; in this situation, a branch can't itself give independent advice, but it can direct customers to the independent arm, or even act as a channel for independent advice as long as it makes no comment on the advice. In some cases, the independent route is pointed out only to customers who have relatively large sums to invest.

Tied agents are regulated by the same rules that apply to a company's own salespeople (see pp.186 to 190), and the company is ultimately responsible for the conduct of its agents. If you deal with tied agents, they must make clear to you their status and the company that they represent. They must follow the 'know your customer' and 'suitable advice' rules, and tied agents who 'cold call' are bound by the regulations outlined on p.189. If you invest through a tied agent, the plan provider will send you details of the product and a cancellation notice (see p.189), giving you 14 days to back out of the deal.

Going to an independent adviser

Getting in touch

If you're unsure which plan provider's products will suit you, it's best to seek help from an independent adviser than from a company salesperson or tied agent.

Local newspapers, trade directories and the *Yellow Pages* may carry advertisements for independent advisers. You may also find some trading in the high street. The titles – 'pensions consultant', 'insurance broker', 'financial adviser', and so on – are often the same as those used by tied agents. Look out for the term 'independent' and also for a round logo with the letters 'IFA'. 'IFA' stands for Independent Financial Adviser and the logo can be used only by independent advisers who have joined IFAP★. This is an organisation set up by a group of insurance companies specifically to provide support and publicity for independent financial advisers. Not all independent advisers have chosen to join IFAP, so the absence of the logo doesn't necessarily mean that a business is not independent. IFAP can provide you with a list of its members in your area.

Many accountants, solicitors and actuaries give financial advice. They are all independent advisers in accordance with the rules governing their professions.

The selling process

As the name suggests, independent advisers are independent of any particular company and must base their advice on the products of the full range of companies in the market.

An independent adviser is bound by the 'know your customer' rule, explained on p.187, and you should expect him or her to investigate all the areas outlined there. An independent adviser must recommend the most suitable product for you from the range available. In practice, the adviser does not have to look at every product on the market for every customer; the adviser must make regular surveys of the market to identify the best products but doesn't need to make a special survey for each customer; the adviser is allowed to identify the 'best' product for an identifiable group – for example, all people in a given age group who want rebate-only pension plans – rather than seeking out a product afresh for each new customer.

If you invest through an adviser, the plan provider will usually send you details of the plan and a cancellation notice – see p.189. You have 14 days to back out of the deal.

How salespeople and advisers are paid

Salespeople employed by a particular company may be paid by salary, bonuses, commission on sales, fringe benefits, such as a car, and so on. Tied agents usually receive commissions on the sales that they make, and they may be able to claim back from the company certain expenses associated with running the business. Most independent advisers receive commission on the sales that they make. In one way or another, the payments to salespeople, agents and independent advisers are met out of charges or expenses on the investment to which you agree. Some agents and advisers charge you a fee for their services and, in this case, commissions they receive may be used to reduce the fee you pay, or the commissions may be paid over to you. Solicitors and accountants always charge fees but may keep any commissions they receive only with your consent.

Payment by commission raises the possibility of some conflict of interest. One potential problem arises with independent advisers. Plan providers compete for the clients of independent advisers, in part, by offering better commission deals than their rivals. Yet, the adviser who is your agent is supposed to advise you with reference only to your circumstances – not to the amount of commission he or she will earn. There is clearly a temptation for an independent adviser to recommend the products of the company that will pay the most commission. Some don't pay commission to the middleman at all, so there's a risk that these plans might be overlooked.

Salespeople and tied agents are, of course, able to sell only the products of one company. But the temptation of commission payments could persuade them – as well as independent advisers – to recommend their customers to invest more than they really wanted to, to recommend a higher-commission product in preference to one which might be more suitable for the customer, or to recommend a product when in fact none of the products available is suitable. You should be on your guard against these problems. Work out for yourself how much you want to invest, make sure that you know what you want and check that the recommended product meets your requirements.

If you use a solicitor or accountant, the problems are less likely to arise because they are bound by the rules of their professions to tell you what commission will be paid to them and, in any case, they can't keep the commission unless you've agreed to that happening. With most other types of independent adviser, you won't necessarily be aware of the commission payment until late in your transaction with the adviser. You'll be sent written details of the amount, or percentage rate, of commission an adviser will receive when the plan provider sends you the full details of the product you've chosen. But these details are sent out after you've agreed the deal, and though you have the 14 days' cancellation period, you're unlikely to alter your choice at that late stage merely because the adviser's commission earnings look a bit high. Instead of waiting, it's a good idea to ask at the time you're discussing the deal with your adviser how much commission he or she stands to earn – an adviser does not have to volunteer this information but *must* provide it *if you ask*.

In 1993, the Office of Fair Trading recommended that commissions should be disclosed at the time you first agree to take out a pension plan. The government agreed and went even further, saying that tied agents, as well as independent advisers, should have to disclose '*at an early stage in the selling process*' how much they stand to receive as a result of arranging your pension plan. The government asked SIB* to work out how this might be done and, at the time of writing, is considering the SIB proposals. Automatic commission disclosure at the time you take out a plan is unlikely to come into effect before the end of 1994.

It's not easy to judge what level of commission is reasonable, but if you're discussing several plans – and with more than one adviser – you'll be alerted to any particularly high payments that might be swaying the recommendation. And high commission payments will generally be passed on to investors, so watch out for high plan charges.

Independent advisers don't have to tell you what commission, if any, they receive through recommending deposit-type plans, such as those which can be (but seldom are) offered by building societies.

Advertisements

The Financial Services Act lays down comprehensive rules to control the way investments are advertised. These include:

- an advertisement must give the name of the advertiser and, usually, the name of the regulating body (see p.159), too
- the nature of the investment must be clear. If full details are not given, the advertisement must say how you can get them
- references to past performance mustn't be misleading, and there must be a warning that past performance isn't necessarily a guide to the future
- projections and illustrations, if used, must be worked out in a set way (see opposite)

- if the value of your investment can go down as well as up – for example, as with unit-linked investments and unit trusts – there must be a warning to this effect.

Information about plans

At the time of writing, new rules are due to be implemented regarding the information you will be given about investment products. When you first approach a plan provider or a middleman for information about pension products, you will probably be offered literature about them, usually in the form of a brochure. When the new rules are operating, either in the brochure or along with it, you must be given details of certain **key features** of the plan in question. It is proposed that the key features covered must include:

- a description of the plan, including the payments which would be required and which, if any, of the benefits are fixed
- if your investment would be unit-linked, details of the funds available
- if your investment would be on a with-profits basis, a description of how the bonuses are worked out
- the risk involved – for example, whether the original value of your capital can fall as well as rise
- a guide to the transfer value of the plan during the first five years, should you decide to switch to another plan
- the effect of charges and expenses on your investment.

The information given in the key features will be based, where necessary, on realistic examples. If you decide to go ahead and invest in the plan, the new rules will require that you be sent broadly the same information again but, this time, including calculations which are based on your specific situation and decisions about, for example, how much to invest. This **important information specific to the investor** (as it is called in the rules) must be sent by the plan provider, unless it can reasonably assume that your adviser has provided the information instead. Where applicable, the important information must also include the note about how much commission your adviser is to receive for arranging the plan for you (see pp.193–95).

Before you decide to take out a particular plan, you will probably like to have an **illustration** (or **projection**) of the possible benefits which you might get from the plan at retirement age. The plan provider or middleman can arrange this. Illustrations are an important tool for your pension planning because they give you a guide to the amount which you need to save, but they should be treated with caution for two reasons. First, an illustration must be based on *assumptions* – educated guesses or estimates – about factors such as future investment performance, a company's expenses, plan charges, and so on. The Financial Services Act requires that illustrations be based on standard assumptions – this guards against individual providers using misleadingly optimistic figures, but it also means that the illustrations are of little help if you want to compare one plan with another. At the time of writing, the growth assumptions to be used in illustrations of pension plans are:

- for a pension plan used solely for contracting out of the State Earnings Related Pension Scheme (SERPS), an investment growth rate up to retirement of either 0.5 per cent or 2.5 per cent. These are projected *real* rates of return – in other words, what you might get over and above the amount needed to keep pace with inflation
- for other plans, an investment growth rate of either 6 per cent or 12 per cent a year up to the time you retire – these are *not* real growth rates.

It must be stressed that these growth rates are not lower and upper limits on the growth you'll experience, they are simply examples of what might happen.

Current illustrations must also use standard assumptions about charges, which means that illustrations from different plan providers will be virtually identical even if one provider, in practice, charges a lot less than another. However, the government has accepted recommendations that, in future, illustrations should be based on a plan provider's own charges and expenses. This means that, at long last, you'll be able to use illustrations as a basis for comparing different plans. At the time of writing, no date had yet been set for the switch to own-charges illustrations. However, regular surveys which already take account of actual charges are published by the specialist magazines *Money Management* and *Pensions Management* (see p.184).

Two other ways of showing charges, which you may come across, are:

- **reduction in premium**   the equivalent deduction from the contribution you paid which would have produced the same reduction in return – shown as so many pence deducted from every £1 of contribution
- **reduction in yield**   the difference between the return expected, taking all charges and expenses into account, and the return you would get if there were no expenses or charges.

The second reason for caution when using illustrations is that, except in the case of contracted-out plans, illustrations generally tell you only what you may eventually get in terms of *future* money – the amounts seem very large (and are often referred to as 'telephone number' figures), but the buying power of each future £1 is almost certainly going to be a lot less than the buying power of £1 today (see p.12). So you must adjust the figures for the likely effect of future inflation before an illustration can be of use. The Financial Services Act requires that you be given a standard note about inflation, but the calculations are not easy for the average person, so ask the plan provider, the agent or your adviser to do the sums for you.

Any illustration you're given must be given in writing – and, if you go ahead with the plan, the provider must keep the illustration on file for at least three years.

Self-defence for shoppers

Though the Financial Services Act provides some very important areas of protection for the investor (see Chapters 11 and 15) – and a limited degree of compensation if things do go wrong – no law can stop the really determined fraudster. You should also take your own protective measures:

- do your homework. Work out roughly what your needs are. Read up to give yourself a broad idea of what's available to meet those needs

- have handy the information you'll need – for example, a recent pay slip, forecast of your state pension, booklet for your employer pension scheme, and so on
- get advice if you need it. With pension problems, solutions are rarely cut and dried, so don't rely on just one adviser – compare the advice of two or three
- don't deal with advisers who are not authorised. With the exception of deposit-type plans (not covered by the Financial Services Act) don't deal with plan providers who are not authorised. Check their status through the SIB* Register (see p.186) *before* you do business with them
- check whether an adviser charges fees. Ask what commissions the adviser will receive
- avoid salespeople and advisers who don't ask enough questions (see p.187) – they can't give sound recommendations if they are ignorant of your circumstances
- get everything in writing – make notes of telephone calls, confirm the contents of meetings in a follow-up letter
- read literature and documents. Make sure you understand them before you agree to invest
- avoid paying money to an adviser. Instead, make cheques payable direct to the plan provider – even if you have to write several cheques for different providers
- keep on file all the information – brochures, notes of meetings, and so on – which formed the basis of your decision to take out a plan.

CHAPTER 15

WHAT TO DO IF THINGS GO WRONG

IF YOU have a problem or complaint concerning your pension arrangements, there are steps you can take to resolve it.

Problems with your state pension

If your complaint concerns your National Insurance contributions record – e.g. you believe that your record is wrong – contact your local DSS office (in the phone book under 'Social Security') and ask for the contributions department; you may be given a form – RD171 – to complete.

With most other complaints concerning your state pension, you should contact your local Benefits Agency (which may be at the same DSS office that deals with contributions, or at a different address). Explain your problem and don't forget to quote your National Insurance number.

If you're not happy with the response from your local office, you can contact the District Manager (the local DSS can tell you the address) or the Chief Executive of the Benefits Agency.

If still not satisfied, write to your MP with your complaint and the response from the DSS. Your MP may refer your case to the Parliamentary Commissioner for Administration (the 'Parliamentary Ombudsman'). You can't contact the Ombudsman yourself.

Problems with personal plans and employer schemes

If you have a complaint concerning your personal pension plan, the plan provider or the advice you were given, you should first ·

contact the manager of the plan provider or the financial adviser with whom you dealt. If you're not satisfied with the response and the company is part of a larger organisation, take your complaint to the head office – the branch you dealt with can tell you whom to contact, or you can get details from a business directory (most public libraries have these).

If you have a complaint concerning your employer pension scheme, contact either the pension scheme administrator or the trustees of the scheme. Details of whom to contact and the address must be included in the basic information about the scheme which you should have been given, and may be displayed on a notice board at work. If you have problems, your firm's personnel department should be able to help.

An advisory scheme

The Occupational Pensions Advisory Service★ (OPAS) was originally set up as a voluntary body to help people who were having problems concerning their employer pension scheme. It has now evolved into a state-backed service with a much wider remit, offering its services to people having problems with either employer schemes or personal plans. The service won't make any judgements about your case, but it can investigate the situation and advise you on the facts relevant to your case. It will often contact the employer scheme or plan provider on your behalf and will try to help you and the scheme or plan provider reach a solution. You can contact OPAS★ direct or through your local Citizens Advice Bureau.

Complaints to the regulator

In the case of personal pension plans, if the pension provider or adviser to whom you complained fails to give a reasonable response, you should write to the relevant Self Regulating Organisation (SRO) or other regulatory body. Summarise the nature of your complaint and the action you've taken so far, including the names and positions of people you've contacted and the relevant dates. The name of the appropriate regulator will be given on the business stationery of the firm. The addresses of the various SROs are given on p.241–43. If the firm you dealt with is a firm of solicitors, accountants, actuaries or insurance brokers the appropriate regulator may be a Recognised Professional Body (RPB) rather than an SRO.

The RPBs are the Chartered Association of Certified Accountants★, Institute of Actuaries★, Institute of Chartered Accountants in England and Wales★, Institute of Chartered Accountants in Ireland★, Institute of Chartered Accountants of Scotland★, Insurance Brokers Registration Council (IBRC)★, The Law Society★, Law Society of Northern Ireland★ and Law Society of Scotland★. The regulator will either deal with your complaint directly or, if possible, pass it to a specialist complaints body.

Specialist complaints bodies

If your complaint concerns a deposit-type personal plan issued by a building society and the society's response to you has not been satisfactory, you can take your complaint to the Office of the Building Societies Ombudsman★. The Ombudsman can investigate the complaint on your behalf, conciliate between you and the society and, in the last resort, act as an arbiter in the dispute by imposing a solution. If – as is more usual – your complaint concerns a personal plan covered by the Financial Services Act, you may also have recourse to an ombudsman or similar scheme. If you've complained to the appropriate regulatory body, it may pass your complaint to the relevant ombudsman or other scheme, but you can contact the ombudsman schemes direct. These bodies will usually try conciliation – i.e. attempt to help you and the pension provider reach a solution – but, if that's unsuccessful, they will judge the case on the basis of the evidence and decide on a solution. These schemes can specify awards to be made to you if they are satisfied that your complaint is valid and that compensation is justified.

The specialist complaints bodies are as follows: the Insurance Ombudsman★ deals with complaints concerning the sale and marketing of plans offered by life insurance companies and unit trusts, provided they are members of the Ombudsman scheme; FIMBRA★ operates its own complaints and arbitration scheme which can be contacted via FIMBRA.

If you have a complaint about a personal pension plan which can't be dealt with by one of the complaints schemes operated by a regulatory body, or if you have a complaint concerning an employer pension scheme and the firm providing the plan or the scheme administrators or trustees have been unable to settle the matter, you can take your problem to OPAS★ (see p.201). If OPAS can't find a solution, you should contact the Pensions Ombudsman★ in writing explaining your problem and enclosing copies of all relevant correspondence with the plan provider or employer scheme. Provided you give your permission, OPAS can release its correspondence with you concerning your case to the Ombudsman. The Pensions Ombudsman can investigate the problem and decide what action is to be taken to set the matter right.

In the case of the Insurance Ombudsman and (usually) the Buildings Society Ombudsman, decisions are not binding on you as complainant – if you disagree with them, you can take your case to court if you wish (see below). By contrast, the decisions of the Pensions Ombudsman are binding on you as well as on the pension plan provider or employer scheme and you *cannot* take the case to court if you're unhappy. The decision of an arbitrator is also binding, so by accepting arbitration, you automatically give up your right to go to court.

Going to court

If the actions of a plan provider, agent or adviser cause you to lose money, you could try to recover your loss by taking the firm to court and suing it for, say, negligence, misrepresentation or breach of the Financial Services Act rules. Similarly, it is possible to take the trustees of an employer pension scheme to court if you believe they have acted against the interests of the scheme members.

However, court cases are generally lengthy, costly and may be difficult to prove, so you'd be wise to look on this course of action as a last resort. If there are other people in the same position as you, you may be able to join together to bring a court action. In a case concerning an employer scheme, you should find out whether a trade union or staff association would be willing to fight the case.

Compensation

If your complaint against a plan provider, agent or adviser is successful and an award is made in your favour – either by the firm itself, through the regulatory body, a specialist complaints procedure or by a court – you'll usually recover your money from the firm. But, sometimes, the firm is broke and can't pay up. In this situation, you may qualify for compensation from one of the industry-wide schemes. If your plan was covered by the Financial Services Act, the Investor Compensation Scheme (ICS) covers the first £30,000 of your investment in full and nine-tenths of the next £20,000 – in other words, the maximum possible compensation is just £48,000. This is the level at which compensation was set when the ICS was first established in 1988 and it has not been increased since. Clearly, it may be entirely inadequate in the case of a claim concerning pension savings.

If your complaint was against an insurance company, you may be covered by the Policyholders' Protection Act scheme, which covers up to nine-tenths of your entitlement without any cash limit.

A claim concerning a deposit-type plan sold by a building society may be covered by the Building Societies Investor Protection Board scheme, which covers nine-tenths of your investment up to £20,000 – a maximum possible of £18,000.

There is, at present, no compensation scheme to pay out if you lose money through an employer scheme. The Pension Law Review Committee (PLRC) – see p.151 – has recommended that such a scheme should be set up to compensate you if you lose out because of fraud, theft or '*other misappropriation*'. At the time of writing, the government was considering what changes might be made to the law in the light of the PLRC recommendations.

CHAPTER 16

ALTERNATIVES TO PENSIONS

ASSUMING you're a taxpayer, pension schemes and plans offer distinct tax advantages over other methods which you could use for saving for retirement because:

- you get tax relief on your contributions
- income and gains from investing the contributions build up tax-free
- you can take part of the benefits in the form of a tax-free lump sum.

On the negative side, pension schemes and plans are inflexible, locking up your money until at least age 50 and, often, later than this. Viewed from one side, this can be a welcome discipline; viewed from the other, it may be a serious disincentive to save. You must be realistic about retirement saving: you need to build up a large sum and you're unlikely to do this if you're constantly dipping into your savings for other reasons. Your money can't do two jobs – it can't be used here and now and also be available at retirement. However, if the way in which pension savings are tied up is putting you off saving for retirement or causing you to save too little, it may be better to consider ways of saving other than through pension schemes and plans – at least for part of your retirement savings.

The best alternatives are investments which still give you some tax advantages – albeit not as great as those you'd get with a pension scheme or plan. The two main contenders are described here.

Personal equity plans (PEPs)

Description

A personal equity plan (PEP) is a long-term investment in shares, unit trusts and/or investment trusts. It is offered by a plan manager, which might, for example, be an insurance company, unit or investment trust company, bank or stockbroker. There are two main types of PEP. With a general PEP, you invest in a spread of shares and/or collective investments (unit trusts and investment trusts). This can give you a balanced spread of risk, which is suitable for retirement saving. With a single company PEP, your investment buys the shares of just one company. This is a high-risk strategy and less suitable for retirement saving.

You can buy and sell shares within your PEP at any time. Either you can make the investment decisions yourself (a **non-discretionary PEP**) or you can leave them to the plan manager, in which case the plan is called a **discretionary PEP**.

Tax position

You don't get any tax relief on the amount you invest, but income and gains earned by the investment *are* tax-free. Dividend income from the investments can be paid out without you losing the tax advantages, so a PEP can be used in two ways: to build up a lump sum for use in retirement; to provide a regular income in retirement. The tax advantages are less advantageous than it may at first seem for most people, because:

- the tax reclaimed on payments to the plan of divided income is limited to 20 per cent from the 1993–94 tax year onwards, and
- you can, in any case, make fairly substantial capital gains each year without having to pay any tax on them (see p.209).

How much you can invest

You can invest up to £6,000 a year in a general PEP and up to £3,000 a year in a single company PEP.

How long you can invest

You can leave your money in a PEP for as long or as short a period as you like, which makes it useful for very long-term saving such as retirement planning.

Risk

This is an investment in the stock market and the value of your shares or units can fall as well as rise. The risk is greater the fewer the number of underlying shares in which you're investing. You can reduce the risk somewhat by choosing a spread of companies; if you invest in a unit trust or investment trust, you will automatically be buying into a spread of different shares and possibly other investments. Over the long term, stock market investments tend to grow faster than inflation, but this isn't guaranteed.

Access to your money

You can withdraw capital at any time without any tax penalty. Dividend income can be paid out tax-free.

Drawbacks

Plan managers levy charges. These may take the form of an initial charge when you invest and possibly an annual charge. You'll have to pay dealing charges too when shares are bought and sold. You may be charged extra for services such as being sent the annual report and accounts of companies in which you hold shares. Charges vary greatly from plan to plan, so check carefully. In the worst cases, plan charges can swallow up most of the tax advantage.

Tax-Exempt Special Savings Accounts (TESSAs)

Description

TESSAs are deposit accounts offered by banks and building societies. You invest for five years and receive interest at a rate which can vary. (A few TESSA providers offer plans with a fixed rate of interest.)

Tax position

There is no tax relief on the amount you invest but interest builds up tax-free. Tax relief may be lost if you don't stick to the rules.

How much you can invest

You can invest up to £3,000 in the first year and up to £1,800 in each subsequent year subject to an overall maximum of £9,000.

How long you can invest

You can invest for only five years, after which the TESSA comes to an end. You would then need to start a new TESSA if you wished to carry on saving in this way.

Risk

The value of your original investment can't fall. Interest, once added, can't be taken away, but the interest rate is usually variable. Interest rates fell sharply during 1993, and over the long term your investment would not normally be expected to keep pace with price inflation.

Access to your money

The tax rules let you take out part of the interest (excluding that amount which corresponds to tax relief at the basic rate) without losing tax relief. However, some TESSA providers don't let you withdraw interest, or impose penalties if you do. You can withdraw your capital at any time but, if you do so before the end of the five year term, all the interest becomes taxable at the basic rate of income tax.

Drawbacks

This method of saving is not suitable for the long term since TESSAs are designed to last only five years and, as with all deposit-based investments, are vulnerable to inflation. However, they can be useful if you are within five years or so of retirement and want a less risky investment than one based on the stock market.

A brief note about tax

Income tax

If you receive income from an investment which is taxable, whether or not you have to pay tax depends on the size of your income from all sources and what deductions you can make from it. The main deduction allowed is your personal allowance and, if you're married, the married couple's allowance (see p.225 for more details about this). The standard rates of allowances in the 1994–95 tax year are:

Personal allowance	£3,445
Married couple's allowance	£1,720

You pay tax at the lower rate of 20 per cent on the first £3,000 by which your income exceeds your allowance(s) and any other deductions. On the next £20,700, you pay tax at the basic rate of 25 per cent. On anything above £23,700, you pay at the higher rate of 40 per cent.

But, for the 1994–95 tax year, the married couple's allowance gives you relief only against tax at the lower rate of 20 per cent – not the basic and higher rates. From 6 April 1995 onwards, this relief will be further restricted to a new level of just 15 per cent, if November 1993 Budget proposals are accepted.

Capital gains tax

You make a gain on an investment when you sell it for more than you originally paid. Gains on some investments are tax-free but, even when this is not the case, all or part of your gain may not be taxable because you can make various adjustments and deductions. First, you can deduct any allowable expenses incurred in the process of buying or selling. Secondly, you can deduct an **indexation allowance**, which reflects that part of the gain which arose as a result of general price inflation (although from 6 April 1995 onwards you cannot use an indexation allowance to create or increase a loss, and from 30 November 1993 until then such losses are restricted to a maximum of £10,000). You can also deduct allowable losses made on other assets you've sold or otherwise disposed of.

After allowing for these deductions, you can make gains of up to £5,800 (in the 1994–95 tax year, assuming November 1993 Budget proposals become law) without having to pay any tax. If you have gains above this amount, tax is worked out by adding your gains to your taxable income. If the income and gains together come to £3,000 or less, tax is charged on the gains at 20 per cent. If the income and gains come to more than £3,000 but less than £23,700, tax on the gain will usually be at 25 per cent (but, if the gain itself takes the amount through the £3,000 threshold, then part of the gain will be taxed at 20 per cent and part at 25 per cent). If the taxable income and gains together come to more than £23,700, tax will usually be charged at 40 per cent (but, if the gain itself takes the amount through the £23,700 threshold, part of the gain will be taxed at 25 per cent and part at 40 per cent).

CHAPTER 17

WHEN YOU RETIRE

RETIREMENT should be a time for relaxing a little, but you may find there's quite a lot of paperwork before you can be sure that your pension income is properly arranged. Here are a few general rules which should help you:

- keep all the documents that you get throughout your working life concerning your pension rights. Don't discard documents relating to your earlier pension schemes and plans
- keep all the papers relating to your pensions in one place – start a file for them, if you haven't one already
- start sorting out your pensions well before your intended retirement date – three to four months before should be adequate in most cases, but allow longer for pensions from any schemes that you left on changing jobs
- always quote relevant reference numbers – for example, your National Insurance number in the case of state pensions, your works number or other scheme reference for an employer scheme, and your policy or plan number with a personal plan – whenever you contact the DSS, a scheme or a plan provider
- keep copies of letters you send
- make notes of telephone calls – include the date, who you spoke to and the main points of the conversation
- once your pensions start to be paid, keep counterfoils, payslips, and so on, in a handy place. You'll need them when you sort out your tax, and you may want them if you have any queries about your pensions.

It's important to keep in touch with old pension schemes and plan providers: if you move or change your name, contact all the relevant schemes and plan providers to give them your new details – it's all too easy to lose touch, only to find you have no idea who'll be paying your pension when you retire.

If you can't track down an old employer from whom you think a pension is due, you can turn to the Pensions Registry for help. The Registry was set up by the government in 1990 to help people trace 'lost' pensions. It holds details of nearly 170,000 employer schemes and, in 1992, it reported that it had successfully helped 87 per cent of the 8,000 people who had so far contacted it. If you need help, complete a Form PR4 which you can get from the Occupational Pensions Advisory Service★ (OPAS) or the Registrar of Pension Schemes★.

Your state pension

How to claim your pension

About four months before you reach the state pension age (currently 60 for women, 65 for men), you should receive a letter from the Department of Social Security (DSS) telling you how much state pension you're entitled to. The pension is *not* paid automatically – you have to claim it, and there should be a claim form (Form BR1) with the letter. Fill this in and return it to the DSS. If you decide to defer your pension (see p.36) and haven't already written to the DSS about this, do so now.

If you haven't heard from the DSS within, say, three months before your birthday, get in touch with them yourself by visiting or writing to your local Benefits Agency. You'll find the address in the telephone book under 'Social Security Department of' or 'Benefits Agency'. Always quote your National Insurance number on any letters you send, and have a note of it with you if you visit the DSS in person.

If you haven't claimed your pension in time for your birthday, don't worry. You can still make your claim after reaching state pension age. A pension for yourself can be backdated up to 12 months. But, if you're a man and you're claiming a pension for your wife based on your own National Insurance (see

Chapter 3), the pension for your wife can be backdated only *six* months – so don't delay too long before making your claim.

Postponing your pension

If you decide to put off the start of your state pension (see p.36) inform the DSS. When you want your pension to start, contact your local DSS and ask for a claim form. You will need a special claim form if you're a man and want the pension to start at age 70, or a woman who wants the pension to start at age 65. If you're younger than this, you'll need Form BR1. You can contact the DSS office which previously handled your pension matters, or get a claim form from your local DSS office.

How your pension is paid

You can choose to have your pension paid weekly by order book, or credited monthly or quarterly to your bank or building society account. If it's paid weekly, you'll be given an order book, rather like a book of cheques already dated and made out to you. You have to nominate a branch of the Post Office at which you'll cash your orders. When you present the book at the post office branch, they will tear out the order for the appropriate week, stamp the counterfoil, and give you your pension.

The pay day for weekly retirement pensions is usually Monday. The pension is paid largely in advance as the pension week runs from Sunday to Saturday. You can't cash the order for a particular week before the date shown on the order, but you can cash it later provided you're still within three months of the date shown. If, for any reason, you haven't cashed an order within the time limit, contact the local Benefits Agency.

EXAMPLE 17.1

George will be 65 in three months' time but he hasn't had any commmunication from the DSS about his retirement pension yet – George has moved around a bit during the last 10 years, so it's possible that the DSS don't have his current address. He decides to write to his local Benefits Agency. He looks up the address in the telephone book, and finds it under 'Benefits Agency'. His letter reads:

The Retreat,
River Walk,
Wincanton,
Somerset BA9 1PJ
1 March 1994

Retirement Pensions Section,
Benefits Agency,
Federated House,
29–31 Hendford,
Yeovil,
Somerset BA20 1SL

National Insurance number: ZB 60 96 24 C

Dear Sir,

Re: <u>retirement pension</u>
I will be 65 on 12 June 1994 and wish to claim my state retirement pension from that date. I've had no communication from the DSS, and I would be grateful if you could send me the appropriate claim form together with details of how much pension I can expect.

Yours faithfully,

George Handy

If you can't get to the post office yourself, someone else can pick up your pension as long as you sign the order (and delete the acknowledgement of receipt). The person collecting your pension must then complete the relevant section on the back of the order. Only hand your order book to someone that you can trust, and make sure it is returned to you promptly.

Instead of weekly payment by order, you can have your pension paid automatically into your personal account (or a joint account that you have with, say, your wife or husband). This can be a bank current or deposit account, a building society savings account, a National Giro current account or a National Savings investment account. Your pension can be credited either four-weekly or thirteen-weekly, and is paid at the end of each four-weekly or quarterly payment period. If you want to have your pension paid direct into your personal account, you should get Leaflet NI105 from the DSS, and complete Form BR436 on the back of the leaflet. Having your pension paid into your bank or building society account is very convenient, although you receive your pension in arrears. If your pension is very small (up to £2 a week) it will normally be paid just once a year either by a crossed order or direct into your account.

However your pension is paid, it's important that you let the DSS know if your circumstances change – for example, if you move, marry or become widowed.

Going abroad

If your pension is paid by weekly order and you go abroad for less than three months, you can simply cash your orders in the normal way when you get back.

If you'll be away for longer, let your Benefits Agency know your plans and choose one of the following arrangements for your pension:

- have it paid into a personal account (see above) while you're away
- ask the DSS to keep the money until you get back and then pay it as a lump sum
- arrange to have the money paid to you abroad.

If your pension is already being paid into a personal account, you don't need to tell your Benefits Agency that you'll be away, unless you'll be gone for more than six months.

If you intend to live abroad in your retirement, then you'll definitely want to arrange to have your pension paid to you in the country in which you choose to live. There is no difficulty in doing this, but if you're abroad at the time of the annual increase in state pensions, you won't qualify for the increase unless you're living in a country which is a member of the Economic Union (EU, formerly called the European Community or EC) or a country with which the UK has an agreement for increasing pensions. These countries include, for example, the Channel Islands, USA and Cyprus, but do not include some popular retirement choices, such as Australia, New Zealand and Canada.

It's very important, therefore, that you check what will happen to your state pension (and entitlement to other state benefits, such as health treatment) before committing yourself to a decision to move abroad. Get in touch with the DSS Overseas Branch*.

Table 17.1: Retiring abroad: useful DSS leaflets

Leaflet number	Leaflet name
NI38	Social security abroad
NI106	Pensioners or widows going abroad
SA4 to SA42	These leaflets outline the special agreements which the UK has with other countries regarding social security payments and state benefits. There is a leaflet for each of Jersey and Guernsey, Australia, Switzerland, New Zealand, Sweden, Malta, Cyprus, Israel, Norway, Yugoslavia, Finland, Canada, Turkey, Bermuda, Iceland, Austria, Jamaica, European Community, USA, Mauritius and The Philippines.

A pension from an employer scheme

How to claim your pension

Different schemes will have different arrangements but here we give a guide to what to expect and what action you should take.

About three months before you reach the normal retirement date (or dates) for any employer schemes that will be paying you a pension, you'll need to be in touch with them. If the schemes haven't contacted you by then, make the first move. Either telephone or write to each scheme asking them to give you the details you need and any forms you must complete. If you're not sure who to contact, telephone and ask who deals with pension matters, or failing that you could address any correspondence to 'The Pensions Administrator' and send it to the employer's normal address (or through the internal post system in the case of your current employer). On your letters, always quote any reference number (check your last Benefit Statement for this), and have your reference number to hand if you telephone. It's a good idea to arrange a meeting with the pensions administrator so that you can discuss your position in detail. Don't be afraid to ask for extra information, or advice.

At this stage, you'll need to ask the following questions about the employer scheme providing your main pension:

- what pension are you entitled to?
- what lump sum are you entitled to?
- will taking a lump sum reduce your pension and, if so, by how much?
- how will the pension be paid; do you have any choices to make about the frequency and method of payment?
- is there a widow's or widower's pension and, if so, how will that affect your retirement pension?
- are there pensions for any other dependants, in the event of your death, and, if so, how much are they?

If you've been making additional voluntary contributions, you'll need to know how much has built up in your fund. If you've been paying into your employer's AVC scheme, then they can tell you how much has built up and how you can use it to enhance your benefits from the main scheme. If you've been paying into a free-standing AVC scheme, you'll have to contact the company or society running the scheme as well as the administrators of your employer scheme.

If you're entitled to a preserved pension (see Chapter 8) from a previous employer scheme, check the documents you have to find out who you should contact: this may be the old scheme, or it may be an insurance company if, say, the old employer scheme no longer exists. You'll need to ask what preserved pension you're entitled to, what other benefits there are, if any, what options you have, and how the pension will be paid.

Retiring early

If you retire earlier than the normal age for your employer scheme you may be able to start receiving a pension even at this earlier date (see Chapter 10). Get in touch with the scheme administrator, relating what you intend. He or she will advise what pension, if any, you qualify for, and any options you have.

If you're intending to retire early because of ill health, first check the rules of your scheme to see if you might qualify for an ill health pension – you'll probably need to look at the detailed rules (ask the pensions administrator or trustees) since scheme booklets often give insufficient detail. Contact the scheme authorities – if possible, *before* your employment stops – to find out what action you'll need to take and what information you'll need to provide. You'll certainly need to provide the scheme with medical evidence – perhaps from the scheme's choice of doctor rather than your own – before a pension can be approved.

Retiring late

Depending on the rules of your employer scheme, you may be able to put off the start of your pension until after the normal retirement age for the scheme. If you want to do this, contact the scheme administrators, telling them what you intend. Ask them to give you details about how long you can defer the pension, and how it will be increased in the interim.

How your pension is paid

Depending on how the pension scheme is arranged, you may get a pension direct from the scheme, or your pension might be provided by an insurance company.

Usually, you'll be able to choose the method of payment which is most convenient for you – for example, a regular cheque through the post or payment direct into a bank or building society account. The scheme rules will generally dictate how often the pension is paid – monthly in advance is common – and when any increases are made. A trivial (i.e. very small) pension – taken to mean less than £260 a year – will generally be converted to a single lump sum at retirement instead of being paid out year by year. In that case, tax at a special rate of 20 per cent will usually be deducted and can't be reclaimed.

A pension from a personal plan

How to claim your pension

About three months before you want your pension to start, get in touch with the pension provider, asking for the details you need and any forms that you must complete. If you had previously selected a retirement date, the provider may contact you; otherwise, you should make the first move. Provided you are within the age limits for receiving a pension from your plan (see p.85), you don't have to actually retire – you can receive a pension but still carry on working.

In any letters, always quote any plan or policy reference number that you've been given. And have the number to hand, if you make contact by telephone. These are the main questions you need to ask the plan provider:

- how much is your pension fund worth?
- how much pension would the plan provider offer?
- can you arrange for your pension to increase each year, and by how much? By how much will your starting pension be reduced to pay for the later increases?
- what's the maximum lump sum you could have, and how much pension would remain? How much as a lump sum do you get for each £1 of pension you give up?
- is there a widow's or widower's pension (or pension for another dependant)? How much must you give up to provide, or increase, a widow's or widower's pension?
- what other options do you have?

When you come to take your pension, you don't usually have to stay with the plan provider with whom you have been saving up until then. Most personal plans include an **open market option** which gives you the right to transfer your pension fund to a different plan provider. Pensions can only be paid by an insurance company or a friendly society – so, if your earlier saving had been made with a unit trust, building society, or bank (unless you dealt with an insurance subsidiary of the society or bank), you will *have* to switch plan provider at retirement. Some insurance companies choose not to concentrate on the actual payment of pensions; their terms tend to be unattractive compared with companies who do specialise in this area, so it's sensible to shop around at retirement and use your open market option if you find a better deal elsewhere.

The **annuity rates** available at the time you retire will have a big impact on the amount of pension you can get. If at the time you want to start taking your pension annuity rates are low, you would be wise to consider putting off your retirement, if you can, until rates are higher. Many personal plans allow you to be flexible about the date from which you start taking your pension, provided you leave it no later than age 75.

If you have protected rights (see Chapter 7) from a contracted-out personal plan, these can – and may have to – be treated quite separately from the rest of your pension. Protected rights can't be paid out until you reach state pension age (65 for men and currently 60 for women), so you'll have to wait for this part of your pension to start if you retire at an earlier age. You must, by law, have an open market option enabling your protected rights pension to be paid by another provider, if you wish.

How your pension is paid

You can usually choose the most convenient method of payment – e.g. direct into a bank or building society account, or by cheque through the post. You may be able to choose whether to have the pension paid, say, monthly, quarterly or only once a year. The pension may be paid in advance or in arrears. You may get slightly more pension if it is paid less frequently, since the pension provider can invest your money in the interim.

A very small pension (provided it's not a protected rights pension) may be paid to you as a single lump sum at retirement.

CHAPTER 18

YOUR TAX IN RETIREMENT

How your pensions are treated for tax

Your state pension

STATE retirement pensions count as part of your income for tax purposes, and you may have to pay tax if your income is high enough (see p.223). The exception is the £10 Christmas bonus, which is tax-free.

The pension is paid without any tax having been deducted, which is convenient if you're a non-taxpayer. If you're a 20 per cent, basic-rate or higher-rate taxpayer, there will be tax to pay. If you're receiving a pension from elsewhere, or you have a job, the tax on your state pension will usually be deducted from the other pension or your earnings through the Pay-As-You-Earn (PAYE) system. If you don't pay the tax due through PAYE, you'll receive an Assessment from the taxman – usually this will give you 30 days within which to pay the tax.

Employer scheme pensions

A pension from an employer scheme is treated as your income for tax purposes, and there will be tax to pay if your income is high enough. Usually, the pension will be paid with tax already deducted through the PAYE system.

PAYE may also be used to collect tax on other parts of your income – for example, tax on your state pension or on income from your investments. This may take you by surprise because it will look as if you're paying too much tax on your employer pension – see the example on p.224. If you're in any doubt about the deductions being made, first check your tax position – ask the employer scheme to help you do this. If you still think you're being over-taxed, contact your tax office.

If, at retirement, you receive a refund of 'excess' additional voluntary contributions (AVCs) – see p.76 – tax will have been deducted at a special rate of 35 per cent. If you're a non-taxpayer or 20 per cent taxpayer, you can't reclaim any of the tax. If you're a basic-rate taxpayer, you're treated as if you've paid tax on the refund at your normal rate – you can't reclaim any of the tax deducted from your refund. If you're a higher-rate taxpayer, you'll have extra tax to pay. The amount you must pay is found by 'grossing up' the net amount of your refund by the basic rate of income tax – this means finding the before-tax amount which would be reduced to the amount of your refund if tax at the basic rate were taken away. Higher-rate tax on the 'grossed up' amount is worked out, but you're deemed to have already paid tax at the basic rate, so your extra tax bill is for the difference between tax at the higher rate and the basic rate – see the example below.

EXAMPLE 18.1

Samuel retired in April 1994 and qualified for a refund of 'excess' AVCs at the time he retired. His refund would have been £1,000, but tax at the special rate of 35 per cent was deducted, so Samuel received 65 per cent of £1,000 = £650.

He's a higher-rate taxpayer, so there will be more tax to pay. This is worked out as follows: £650 grossed up at the basic rate of tax (25 per cent in the 1994–95 tax year) is £650 ÷ (1−0.25) = £867. Tax at the higher rate (40 per cent) would be 0.40 × £867 = £347. Samuel is deemed to have already paid tax at the basic rate which would be 0.25 × £867 = £217. So he must pay extra tax of £347 − £217 = £130.

Personal pensions

A personal pension counts as your income for tax purposes, so there will be tax to pay if your income is high enough. The pension provider will usually deduct tax through PAYE before handing over the pension to you.

Using the PAYE system, tax on any other income you have – for example, a state pension – may also be deducted from your personal plan before it is paid. This may mislead you into thinking that you're paying too much tax on your personal plan. Before taking any other action, check your full tax position (see below) and the total tax you're paying. If you still find that your tax bill is too high, contact your tax office.

Your tax in retirement

In retirement, your tax bill continues to be worked out in the normal way, but you may benefit from higher tax allowances, so there may be less tax to pay than when you were working, even if your income stays the same. The calculations below are carried out for each **tax year**, which runs from 6 April in one year to 5 April in the next. Your tax bill is worked out like this:

- **income** – except for any tax-free income, such as the first £70 interest from a National Savings ordinary account, or the proceeds on maturity from most regular-premium insurance policies – from all sources is added together. This will include your pensions, interest earned by any investments, earnings from any work you do, and so on
- **outgoings** which you pay in full are subtracted from your income. 'Outgoing' is tax jargon for any expenses which qualify for tax relief – with some you get relief by paying a 'net' amount from which the tax relief has already been deducted. Outgoings include interest payments on the first £30,000 of any mortgage you have (though relief is restricted to 20 per cent in April 1994–95, and will be further limited to 15 per cent from 6 April 1995 assuming November 1993 Budget proposals are passed), pension contributions if you're still making them, and donations you make to charity under a deed of covenant. Income less outgoings is called your total income

- **allowances** are then subtracted. Traditionally, an allowance has been a slice of income on which you don't pay tax. Everyone (even a child) has a personal allowance and some people – for example, married couples – qualify for extra allowances. In a departure from tradition, from 1994–95, the tax relief given through the married couple's allowance (and some other allowances related to it) is restricted to just the 20 per cent rate, even if your top rate of tax is higher. The tax relief given by these allowances will be further restricted – see p.226 – if November 1993 Budget proposals become law
- what's left is your **taxable income**. This is divided into three slices. On the first slice of £3,000 in 1994–95, you pay tax at 20 per cent. On the second slice, called the **basic rate band**, you pay tax at the basic rate. On anything more, you pay tax at a higher rate. In the 1994–95 tax year, the basic rate band runs from taxable income of £3,000 to £23,700 and the basic tax rate is 25 per cent. The higher tax rate is 40 per cent.

EXAMPLE 18.2

Charlotte, 66, has the following income in the 1994–95 tax year: state pension of £2,995, employer pension of £2,200, income from National Savings Pensioners Guaranteed Income Bonds of £1,400 and income of £1,600 from the ordinary National Saving Income Bonds. During the year, she pays gross interest of £600 on a small mortgage, but has no other outgoings. Her 'total income' is £7,595. She has a personal allowance of £4,200 (see p.225) which leaves her a taxable income of £3,395. The first £3,000 of this is taxed at a rate of 20 per cent – i.e. tax of £600. The remaining £395 is taxed at the basic rate of 25 per cent – i.e. tax of £98.75. In total, her tax bill for 1994–95 is £698.75.

She receives her state pension and her investment income without tax having been deducted, so the whole tax bill is collected from her employer pension through the PAYE system. This makes it look as if her employer pension is being taxed at a rate of nearly 32 per cent (£698.75 as a proportion of £2,200). But this isn't really the case, because the tax deducted was the amount due on *all* her income, not just the employer pension.

Bank and building society interest

Bank and building society interest is now usually paid out, or credited to your account, after tax at the basic rate has been deducted. If you're a basic-rate taxpayer, this is very convenient as you have no further tax to pay. If you're a higher-rate taxpayer, there is extra tax due – you'll need to 'gross up' the interest to find out how much to pay – see Example 18.3. If you're a 20 per cent taxpayer, you can reclaim part of the tax deducted.

If you're a taxpayer, you can reclaim *all* tax deducted, or, better still, arrange to receive the interest gross, i.e. without tax deducted. To receive gross interest, fill in form R85, from banks, building societies, tax offices or post offices, to certify that you are eligible, then hand it in to your bank or building society. If you have a joint account with a taxpayer, you can still usually receive your half of the interest before the deduction of tax.

EXAMPLE 18.3

Christian, who is a higher rate taxpayer, receives £3,561 interest from his building society account in the 1994–95 tax year. This is 'net' interest – i.e. the amount left after tax at the basic rate has been deducted. To find the 'gross' (before-tax) amount of interest which this is equivalent to, he must work out the following sum: £3,561 ÷ [1 – 0.25%] = £3,561 ÷ 0.75 = £4,748 The higher rate of tax is 40 per cent, so tax on £4,748 is 0.4 × £4,748 = £1,899.20. However, Christian has already paid basic-rate tax of 0.25 × £4,748 = £1,187, so he has only to pay the remaining £1,899.20 – £1,187 = £712.20.

Your tax allowances in retirement

Everyone has a personal tax allowance. In the 1994–95 tax year, the personal allowance for most people is £3,445. But, if you're aged 64 or over on the first day of the tax year, you qualify for a higher personal allowance, the age allowance. There are two rates: in the 1994–95 tax year, the allowance is £4,200 for people aged 64 to 73 at the start of the tax year, and the higher age allowance is £4,370 for people aged 74 or more.

A husband and wife each get a personal allowance to set against their own income. But they also get an extra allowance called the **married couple's allowance**. In the 1994–95 tax year, the ordinary married couple's allowance is £1,720. If either husband or wife (or both) are aged 64 or over on the first day of the tax year, a higher married couple's age allowance is payable. In 1994–95, this is £2,665 if the husband or wife was aged 64 to 73 at the start of the tax year and £2,705 if aged 74 or over.

While the personal allowance saves you tax at your highest rate, the married couple's allowance only gives you tax relief at a rate of 20 per cent in the 1994–95 tax year, and 15 per cent from 6 April 1995 onwards (regardless of your top rate of tax).

From 6 April 1990 to 5 April 1993, it was usual for the husband to receive the married couple's allowance, although if he didn't have enough income to make full use of the allowance, the excess could be transferred to his wife. From 1993–94 onwards, a wife can elect to claim half the married couple's allowance (but only the basic amount, not including any age-related increase) to set against her own income – the husband then keeps just the other half. Or, the husband and wife may elect jointly that the wife will have the whole allowance (the husband then has the right to claim half of it if he wishes). And, if either husband or wife has too little income to make full use of the whole or part of the married couple's allowance (including, in the case of the husband, the age-related increase) which they receive, the excess can be transferred to the other partner.

Thus, in 1994–95, it would be worth transferring the allowance to the wife if she pays tax at 20 per cent or a higher rate and the husband is a non-taxpayer.

Income limit for age allowance

Age allowances are reduced for people with earnings above a certain level. The personal age allowance is reduced if you have 'total income' (see p.223) of more than £14,200 in the 1994–95 tax year. The married couple's age allowance is reduced if the person receiving it has income over £14,200 in the 1994–95 tax year. In either case, the allowance is reduced by £1 for every £2 of income above the limit, but the reduction stops once the allowances have fallen to the amounts that people under age 64 receive. So, whatever your income, in the 1994–95 tax year, your personal allowance could not be less than £3,445 and the married couple's allowance couldn't be less than £1,720.

EXAMPLE 18.4

Mary and Denis have been married for nearly 40 years. Mary is 66 and qualifies for a personal age allowance of £4,200 in the 1994–95 tax year. Denis is 62. He's too young to get personal age allowance and gets the normal personal allowance of £3,445. But he also receives the married couple's allowance and this is set initially at the higher level of £2,665 because of Mary's age.

Denis, however, hasn't retired yet and earns £14,700 a year – £500 above the £14,200 limit for age allowance. This means that the married couple's age allowance is reduced by £250 (£1 for each £2 of the excess income). Denis' married couple's age allowance becomes £2,665 − £250 = £2,415. This is still more than the normal allowance of £1,720.

Mary's personal age allowance is not affected by Denis' earnings, and her own income is less than the £14,200 limit.

CHAPTER 19

MAKING YOUR PENSION CHOICE

THERE are many factors to consider when deciding how best to save for retirement. Which course of action is right for you will depend on your own particular circumstances and, where an employer scheme is available, on the particular features of that scheme. Here, we pull together the choices you're most likely to face, and summarise the main points to consider in each case.

Employees: should you contract out of SERPS?

1. Advantages of SERPS: the pension is inflation-proofed before and after retirement; the pension is a predictable amount in relation to your pre-retirement earnings.
2. Disadvantages of SERPS; government has reduced pensions for future pensioners and could again. If you're young, paying towards SERPS may not give good value for money.
3. Assuming future investment growth is moderate, men and women up to the age of 30 are probably better off contracted out of SERPS. If you qualify for the one per cent extra incentive from the DSS, then you may be better off contracted out up to your late thirties (women) and 40 (men). Beyond these ages, the position is less clear cut, but the older you get the more likely it is that you should either stay in SERPS or contract back into it.
4. Whatever your age, being contracted-out through an employer final pay scheme currently can't reduce your pension compared with staying in SERPS. However, the government is reviewing the link between these schemes and SERPS.

5. You can contract out of SERPS without leaving a contracted-in employer scheme. A rebate-only personal plan is a better route for contracting out than a free-standing additional voluntary contribution scheme.

6. Don't leave a good employer scheme simply to contract back into SERPS – you'll lose more than you gain.

Employees: employer scheme or personal plan?

All schemes

1. If the employer scheme is a non-contributory one, it will be worth joining unless it provides a poor package of benefits. Don't be tempted to think that any benefits are a good thing if you have nothing to pay: joining the employer scheme will prohibit you from making better pension provision through your own personal plan.

2. Your employer must contribute towards the employer pension scheme. Relatively few employers are prepared to contribute towards a personal plan.

3. The administration costs per member of the employer scheme are likely to be significantly lower than the charges set against a personal plan. So, in a money purchase employer scheme, more of the contributions are left to be invested for your pension and other benefits – and, in some schemes, the employer will meet the costs separately, leaving the whole of the contributions to be invested. (In an employer final pay scheme your benefits are set independently of the running costs of the scheme).

4. Your employer probably provides a whole package of benefits: retirement pension, help if you become ill, and help for your family in the event of your death. Would at least some benefits – for example, lump sum life cover – continue if you left the pension scheme? Could you afford to secure comparable benefits through a personal plan? On the other hand, do you need all the benefits? Personal plans let you tailor the benefits to your needs.

5. If you contribute to the employer scheme, you have to pay in a set amount or a set proportion of your earnings each pay

period – monthly, say. Contributing to a personal plan can give you more flexibility over what you pay and when.

6. If you leave your employer scheme now, could you rejoin later if you wanted to?

Final pay schemes

1. If you're within 10 or 20 years of retirement, your employer may be contributing substantially towards your pension through payments to the employer scheme. Would your employer contribute to your personal plan? If you're young and likely to change jobs a few times, you might not get much benefit from your employer contributions to the employer scheme. It won't matter so much if he or she won't contribute to your personal plan.

2. If you stay with the employer scheme for many years, you have the security of knowing that your pension is growing in line with your earnings. This makes final pay schemes particularly attractive if you're an older employee, or if you expect to make a career within one company.

3. You know that your pension will be a predictable proportion of your pre-retirement earnings. This makes it fairly easy for you to judge if your retirement income will be adequate and to plan extra savings, if you feel that is necessary.

4. If you change jobs soon after joining the scheme, the benefits might not add up to much. If you expect to change jobs several times, final pay schemes may not be best for you. So, if you're in the early stages of your career, or if you're a woman who expects to take career breaks because of family commitments, a personal plan might be more suitable.

Money purchase schemes

1. Changing jobs shouldn't affect the money purchase pension you've already built up because the contributions already paid in continue to be invested as before. And, given the other advantages of employer schemes (see above), joining your employer money purchase scheme is likely to be a better option than taking out a personal plan.

Running your own company: executive plan or personal plan?

1. In your role as employer, you can pay large amounts into an executive plan (provided you stay within the Inland Revenue benefit limits), whereas there are limits on the contributions paid into a personal plan. So an executive plan may give you more scope for building up a pension fast or providing a wide range of benefits (though the Inland Revenue is proposing changes which would reduce somewhat the amount which can be invested in an executive plan).

2. There's no limit to the benefits from a personal plan (except a cash ceiling on the tax-free lump sum for some old-style plans). There is a limit on the benefits from an executive plan. Once the benefit limits are reached, there's no point making further contributions. For plans taken out on or after 14 March 1989 (or which you joined on or after 1 June 1989), the benefit limits will be particularly irksome if you earn more than the limit – £76,800 a year for the 1994–95 tax year.

3. The benefit limits – which are defined in terms of your **final pay** – can be a problem if your earnings fall considerably in the last decade or so before retirement.

4. By varying your employer contributions to an executive plan, you currently have a flexible tool for helping you to minimise your tax bill – though limits on contributions may be introduced in future. Personal pension plans can also be used in tax planning but to a lesser extent because of the limit on contributions.

Self-employed: old-style plan or new?

1. If you have an old-style plan and you're not using your full contributions limit, you can take out a new-style plan as well. But you'll often pay less in charges if you contribute to just one plan.

2. If you're considering giving up your old-style plan in favour of a new-style plan, consider these points:
   - with a new-style plan you can start your pension from age 50; with an old-style plan, you must wait until 60

- with an old-style plan, you can usually take a larger tax-free lump sum – up to three times the remaining pension. With a new-style plan, you can take only a quarter of the value of your fund. Switching to a new-style plan means you'll have to settle for the lower lump sum. (But bear in mind that if you exercise an open market option under the old-style plan, you'll be bound by the new-style plan limits anyway).

- you don't have to decide now. You can take a transfer value from your old-style plan at any time before retirement and pay it into a new-style plan. You could even leave this decision until just before you want to start taking a pension.

At retirement: a lump sum from your employer scheme or personal plan?

1. It's nearly always worthwhile taking the maximum possible lump sum, because the lump sum is tax-free, whereas your pension counts as taxable income.
2. You'll almost certainly be worse off if you decide to give up pension from a scheme which *tends* to inflation-proof pensions, but without actually *guaranteeing* to do this.
3. If taking a lump sum leaves you with less pension than you need, consider using the lump sum to buy a lifetime annuity. This is more tax-efficient than not taking the lump sum at all, because the whole of the pension you give up is treated as income for tax purposes. But part of the 'income' from a purchased life annuity is treated as the return of your original investment and is tax-free; the remainder is taxable. However, bear in mind that annuity rates vary. If rates are low at the time you need to buy, you'll be stuck with a low pension – if possible, wait for annuity rates to recover.

GLOSSARY OF PENSIONSPEAK

IT'S VIRTUALLY impossible to consider your pension position without stumbling over a vast array of pensions jargon. Some of this has been created by the state as a product of legislation and regulation; some has been created by the pensions industry itself. Unfortunately, not content with just one word for each concept, there are sometimes two or three terms for the same thing. Jargon has its use as a shorthand for long-winded, and sometimes complex, ideas, but it can be daunting for the non-expert. This glossary attempts to enlighten even the most confused. It brings together many of the technical terms introduced in this book and other terms that you're likely to come across during your pension planning.

Accrual rate The rate at which you build up pension in a final pay pension scheme. Usually expressed as a fraction of final pay – for example, sixtieths, eightieths or hundredths

Actuary A professional person who is expert at calculating probabilities and future values from available statistical, and other, data. Often, employed in the field of pensions and insurance

Additional pension Pension from the *State Earnings Related Pension Scheme* plus any *guaranteed minimum pensions* you qualify for

Additional voluntary contributions (AVCs) Contributions you choose to make to boost your pension and other benefits from a particular employer pension scheme

Annuity A regular income – for example, paid monthly – which you get in exchange for a lump sum. You can't get your original capital back as a lump sum. The income from an annuity may be a fixed amount, or it may increase (or decrease). Increasing annuities are generally the most useful form for providing, or supplementing, retirement income. An annuity may pay an income for life or, in the case of a 'temporary annuity', just for a specified number of years

Annuity rate   A way of expressing the amount of income you get from an annuity as a proportion of the lump sum you invest. Where the income from an annuity increases (or decreases), the annuity rate tells you the proportion the starting income bears to the lump sum invested

Appropriate personal pension   A personal pension plan which can be used to contract out of SERPS

AVC   See *additional voluntary contributions*

Basic pension   The main state pension paid at a single flat level regardless of your earnings. If you don't have enough National Insurance contributions to qualify for the full rate, you might qualify for a pension at a reduced rate

Benefits   What you get out of a pension scheme or plan. This may include retirement pension, a lump sum at retirement, widow's and widower's pensions, pensions for children, pensions on retirement through ill health, increases to pensions, and lump sum life insurance

Benefits Agency   A part of the Department of Social Security which deals with the administration of most social security benefits

Benefit statement   A statement, provided by an employer pension scheme, showing the pension and other benefits you've built up so far, and what you can expect by the normal retirement age

Buy out bond   Another name for a *Section 32 plan*

Class 1 contributions   National Insurance paid by employees, which count towards the full range of contributory state benefits – for example, basic retirement pension and SERPS pension, sick pay, maternity benefits, and unemployment benefit. Employers also pay Class 1 contributions on behalf of each employee

Class 2 contributions   National Insurance paid by the self-employed. These count towards state retirement pensions and sickness benefit, but they don't count towards sick pay, maternity pay, unemployment benefit or SERPS pensions

Class 3 contributions   National Insurance that you can choose to pay to fill gaps in your National Insurance record for the purpose of qualifying for state basic pension (and widow's benefits)

Class 4 contributions National Insurance paid by the self-employed. They are a straight tax and don't entitle you to any benefits

Commutation Exchanging part of your pension at retirement for a tax-free lump sum. Inland Revenue rules dictate the maximum lump sum you can have, and this varies according to the type of scheme or plan that you have and when you started to pay into it.

Compound interest Interest which is added to the original capital sum, and itself grows as interest on the interest is added

COMPS Abbreviation for *contracted-out money purchase scheme*

Contracted-out money purchase scheme An employer money purchase pension scheme which must provide a pension at state pension age, and a widow's or widower's pension, which you receive instead of SERPS benefits you would otherwise have got. Your entitlement to these benefits is sometimes called your *protected rights*. The scheme may also aim to provide you with pension and other benefits in excess of your protected rights

Contracting out Giving up part of your SERPS pension and getting instead a pension, and other benefits, from an employer pension scheme or a personal pension plan

Contributions What your employer, you, and sometimes the government, pay into a pension scheme or plan. Contributions to the state schemes are called National Insurance contributions

Deferred pension An imprecise term often used as another name for a *preserved pension*. It can also mean a pension which will start to be paid after the normal retirement date for a plan or scheme

Department of Social Security (DSS) The government department dealing with pensions, among other matters

Deposit administration scheme Type of pension plan or fund provided by many insurance companies in which your contributions grow by earning interest. Once added, the amount of interest can't be taken away, though future interest rates can change

Deposit-based pension plan Type of personal pension plan sometimes offered by building societies in which your contributions grow by earning interest. Once added, the amount of interest can't be taken away, though future interest rates can change. Banks can also offer deposit-based plans, though, at the time this book went to press, none chose to do so

DHSS Abbreviation for Department of Health and Social Security – an old government department which covered pensions, among other matters

DSS   See *Department of Social Security*

Dynamisation   The process of increasing previous years' earnings in line with inflation in order to boost the value of final pay used to calculate Inland Revenue limits on pension and other benefits from employer pension schemes

Employer pension scheme   Scheme run by an employer to provide employees with a pension at retirement and, usually, other benefits as well

Escalation   A term often used to indicate a system of increasing a pension once it starts to be paid

Final pay scheme   Also called a 'defined benefit scheme'. Type of pension scheme in which the retirement pension and some other benefits are related to your pay near retirement (or when you leave the scheme, if this is before retirement) and the number of years for which you've been a member of the scheme

Free-standing additional voluntary contributions (FSAVCs) Contributions you choose to make to an AVC plan which is independent of your employer pension scheme, while still a member of the employer scheme. The proceeds of the plan must be used to boost the benefits from the employer scheme

FSAVC   See *free-standing additional voluntary contributions*

GMP   See *guaranteed minimum pension*

Graduated pension   Relatively small earnings-related pension from an old state pension scheme

Guaranteed minimum pension (GMP) the amount by which your State Earnings Related Pension Scheme (SERPS) pension is reduced if you are contracted out. Also the minimum amount of pension you receive at retirement from an employer final pay scheme in respect of periods for which you were contracted out. An employer final pay scheme must also provide guaranteed minimum pensions for widows and widowers

Home responsibilities protection   Scheme to protect your entitlement to your state pensions while you are caring for someone at home – for example, children or an elderly relative

Hybrid schemes   Employer pension schemes which work out pensions, and other benefits, on an alternative of final pay and money purchase bases, and give you whichever is the better

Inflation   Sustained increase in price or earnings levels, commonly measured by changes in the Retail Prices Index (price inflation) or changes in the index of National Average Earnings (earnings inflation)

Inland Revenue Government department dealing with, among other things, income tax affairs

Lower earnings limit Minimum level of earnings set each year to determine the point at which National Insurance starts to be paid, and used in the calculation of entitlement to various benefits. (It is approximately equal to the single person's rate of state basic pension)

MAPP See *minimum appropriate personal pension*

Married women's reduced rate contributions A lower rate of Class 1 National Insurance paid by some married women and widows. These contributions do not build up any rights to state pensions

Middle band earnings Also known as 'upper band earnings'. Earnings above the *lower earnings limit* and up to the *upper earnings limit*

Minimum appropriate personal pension (MAPP) Another name for a *rebate-only personal pension plan*

Money purchase scheme Also known as a 'defined contribution scheme'. Pension scheme or plan in which the amount of the eventual pension and other benefits depends on the amount contributed, how invested contributions grow, and *annuity rates* at the time of retirement

NAPF survey An annual survey of employer pension schemes in the UK carried out for the National Association of Pension Funds

National Insurance System of contribution payments which entitles you to specific state pensions and other state benefits. The exceptions to this are Class 4 National Insurance and employers' Class 1 National Insurance on earnings above the *upper earnings limit*, which are straightforward taxes which carry no benefit entitlement at all

National Insurance Credits Class 1 (or occasionally Class 3) National Insurance contributions that you are deemed to have made, though you have not actually paid them. You are entitled to credits in specified circumstances, such as sickness, unemployment, training and pregnancy. Class 1 credits count as National Insurance only at the minimum levels – in other words, as if you had earnings equal to the *lower earnings limit*

National Insurance rebate Part of your, and your employer's National Insurance which the DSS pays to a *personal pension plan*, and which must be used to provide *protected rights*. Also the amount by which National Insurance contributions are reduced if you are contracted out through an employer scheme, and the minimum amount which must be paid into a contracted-out money purchase scheme

Occupational pension scheme Another name for an *employer pension scheme*

Pension A regular income, usually paid for life

Personal pension plan Money purchase-type pension scheme run by an insurance company, friendly society, unit trust, building society or bank. It aims to provide you with a pension at retirement and possibly other benefits. A personal plan need not be connected with a specific job

Plan provider A company, society or other institution which operates personal pension plans. Can be an insurance company, friendly society, unit trust, bank or building society

Preserved pension The pension you're entitled to receive at retirement from a pension scheme, or plan, to which contributions for you are no longer being paid

Protected rights Pension and widow's or widower's pension which must be provided as a result of investing the *National Insurance rebate* in a *personal pension plan*

Rebate-only plan Personal pension plan used to contract out of the *State Earnings Related Pension Scheme* (SERPS). It accepts only the *National Insurance rebate*, together with basic rate tax relief, and any incentive, if applicable. These must be used solely to provide *protected rights* when the plan holder reaches *state pension age*

Reduction in premium (RIP) Method of expressing the amount by which all the various charges and expenses reduce the return you'll get from a pension plan or certain other investments. It is expressed as the number of pence which would have to be deducted from each £1 of premium you pay to cover all the charges and expenses if they were deducted at the outset

Reduction in yield (RIY) Method of expressing the amount by which all the various charges and expenses reduce the return you'll get from a pension plan or certain other investments. It is expressed as the difference between the percentage per annum return you'd get if there were no charges and the percentage per annum return you'd get taking all charges into account

Retail Prices Index (RPI)   Government measure of the average price level in the UK. Changes in the index are commonly used as a measure of price inflation

Retirement Pensions Forecast and Advice Service   Government computerised service for telling you what is your current, and possible future, entitlement to state pensions.

RPI   See *Retail Prices Index*

Section 32 plan   Special plan for receiving transfer values from an employer pension scheme to which you have ceased making contributions. Also called a *buy-out plan*

Section 226 plan   Former name for a *section 620 plan*

Section 620 plan   Old-style personal pension plan superseded from 1 July 1988 by new-style personal pension plans. Can't be used for contracting out of SERPS

Section 621 policy   Life insurance policy which you can take out if you're eligible for an old-style personal pension plan. Broadly, the same as a section 637 policy

Section 637 policy   Life insurance policy which you can take out if you're eligible for a new-style personal pension plan. Premiums, up to 5 per cent of your pensionable earnings or profits, qualify for tax relief at your top rate of tax. But the premiums count towards your overall pension contribution limit

SERPS   See *State Earnings Related Pension Scheme*

State Earnings Related Pension Scheme (SERPS)   Part of the state pension scheme which began in 1978 and which pays earnings-related pensions. If you work for an employer, you can be contracted out of this part of the state scheme

State pension age   Earliest age at which you become eligible to receive a pension from the state (and/or related pensions paid by contracted-out employer schemes and personal plans). Currently, this age is 65 for men and 60 for women. For women born after 5 April 1950, the state pension age is to increase progressively until it reaches 65 – i.e. the same as for men – for all women retiring from 2020 onwards

Transfer value   Lump sum deemed to have the same value as the pension, and any other benefits, that you are entitled to from a scheme or plan to which you've ceased making contributions. The transfer value is paid into another plan or scheme, subject to some restrictions in respect of *guaranteed minimum pensions* and *protected rights*

Unitised with-profits plan   Pension plan offered by some insurance companies in which your contributions are allocated to a fund whose value is linked to the growth of the company's investments and other factors affecting the company's overall profitability. You also receive bonus units at intervals. The value of your units can't fall, but future increases and bonus units are not guaranteed

Unit-linked plan   Pension plan offered by many insurance companies in which the value of your invested contributions is linked to a specific fund of investments. The value of your plan can do down as well as up

Unit trust plan   Pension plan offered by some unit trusts in which contributions are used to buy a stake (in the form of a number of 'units') in a specific pool of investments. The value of your plan depends on the performance of the underlying investments, and can go down as well as up

Upper band earnings   See *middle band earnings*

Upper earnings limit   Maximum level of earnings set each year, on which employees (but not employers) pay National Insurance. Also used in the calculation of entitlement to the *State Earnings Related Pension Scheme* pension and the *National Insurance rebate*

With-profits plan   Pension plan provided by insurance companies. The return on contributions depends on the performance of the insurance company, reflecting factors such as investment performance, expenses, profit-distribution policy and so on. Your return is in the form of bonuses which are added to your plan at intervals, and when the plan comes to an end. Once added, bonuses can't be taken away

Working life   Officially defined by the state and used to calculate your entitlement to basic pension. For most people it means the tax years from age 16 to just before reaching state pension age – currently 44 years for a woman, and 49 for a man. From 2020, women will also have a working life of 49 years

Addresses

Association of British Insurers
51 Gresham Street
London EC2V 7HQ
Tel 071–600 3333

Association of Consulting
  Actuaries
1 Wardrobe Place
London EC4V 5AH
Tel 071–248 3163

Building Societies Ombudsman
Grosvenor Gardens House
35-37 Grosvenor Gardens
London SW1X 7AW
Tel 071–931 0044

Chartered Association of
  Certified Accountants
29 Lincoln's Inn Fields
London WC2A 3EE
Tel 071–242 6855

Consumers' Association
  (book orders)
Dept SSW
PO Box 44
Hertford X
SG14 1SH
Freephone (0800) 252100

Consumer's Association
  (Which? subscriptions)
Subscriptions Dept
PO Box 44
Hertford X
SG14 1SH
Freephone (0800) 252100

Department of Social Security
  (DSS)
*To check contributions, request a
  pension forecast and other queries,
  contact your local DSS office or
  Benefits Agency – in the phone
  book under 'Social Security,
  Department of' or 'Benefits
  Agency'. If you live or work
  overseas, contact:*
DSS Overseas Branch
Benton Park Road
Newcastle-upon-Tyne NE98 1YX
Tel 091–213 5000

DSS Benefits Agency
  (Chief Executive)
286 Euston Road
London NW1 3DN

DSS Freeline Social Security
*This free telephone enquiry service is
available in several languages:*
English (0800) 666555
Chinese (0800) 252451
Punjabi (0800) 521360
Urdu (0800) 289188
Welsh (0800) 289011
also Northern Ireland
(0800) 616757

DSS leaflets
*from DSS offices, some post offices,
public libraries, or from:*
BA Storage and Distribution
Centre
Manchester Road
Heywood
Lancs OL10 2PZ

Financial Intermediaries,
Managers and Brokers
Regulatory Association
(FIMBRA)
Hertsmere House
Hertsmere Road
London E14 4AB
Tel 071–538 8860 *or* 071–895 1229

FT Business Enterprises Ltd
(publishers of *Money
Management* and *Pensions
Management*)
Garrard House
2–6 Homesdale Road
Bromley, Kent BR2 9WL
Tel 081–402 8485

IFAP
*For a list of independent financial
advisers in your area:*
Tel (0483) 461461

Institute of Actuaries
Staple Inn Hall
High Holborn
London WC1V 7QJ
Tel 071–242 0106

Institute of Chartered
Accountants in England and
Wales
PO Box 433
Chartered Accountants' Hall
Moorgate Place
London EC2P 2BJ
Tel 071–920 8100

Institute of Chartered
Accountants in Ireland
Chartered Accountants' House
87–89 Pembroke Road
Dublin 4
Eire
Tel (010) 3531 6680400

Institute of Chartered
Accountants of Scotland
27 Queen Street
Edinburgh EH2 1LA
Tel 031–225 5673

Insurance Brokers Registration
Council
15 St Helen's Place
London EC3A 6DS
Tel 071–588 4387

Insurance Ombudsman's Bureau
135 Park Street
London SE1 9EA
Tel 071–928 7600

Investment Management
Regulatory Organisation
(IMRO)
Broadwalk House
6 Appold Street
London EC2A 2LL
Tel 071–628 6022

Investors Compensation Scheme
Gavrelle House
2–14 Bunhill Row
London EC1Y 8RA
Tel 071–628 8820

The Law Society
113 Chancery Lane
London WC2A 1PL
Tel 071–242 1222

Law Society of Northern Ireland
Law Society House
98 Victoria Street
Belfast BT1 3JZ
Tel (0232) 231614

Law Society of Scotland
Law Society Hall
26 Drumsheugh Gardens
Edinburgh EH3 7YR
Tel 031–226 7411

Life Assurance and Unit Trust
Regulatory Organisation
(LAUTRO)
Centre Point
103 New Oxford Street
London WC1A 1QH
Tel 071–379 0444

Occupational Pensions Advisory
Service (OPAS)
11 Belgrave Road
London SW1V 1RB
Tel 071–233 8080

Pensions Ombudsman
11 Belgrave Road
London SW1V 1RB
*Note that you must let OPAS (see
p.201) try to resolve your problem
before you contact the Pensions
Ombudsman*

Registrar of Pension Schemes
Occupational Pensions Board
PO Box 1NN
Newcastle-upon-Tyne NE99 1NN
Tel 091–225 6393/4

Securities and Futures Authority
(SFA)
Cottons Centre
Cottons Lane
London SE1 2QB
Tel 071–378 9000

Securities and Investments Board
(SIB)
Gavrelle House
2-14 Bunhill Row
London EC1Y 8RA
Tel 071–638 1240
SIB register inquiries
Tel 071–929 3652

Society of Pension Consultants
(SPC)
Ludgate House
Ludgate Circus
London EC4A 2AB
Tel 071–353 1688

INDEX